Resolving Conflicts:

A HANDBOOK FOR STUDENTS

GLOBE FEARON
Pearson Learning Group

Project Editors: Laura Baselice, Lynn W. Kloss, Keisha Carter
Editorial Development: WordWise, Inc.
Production Manager: Penny Gibson
Production Editor: Nicole Cypher
Marketing Managers: Nancy Surridge, Sandra Hutchison
Interior Electronic Design: Kilcullen Design
Illustrator: Allen Davis
Photo Research: PhotoSearch
Electronic Page Production: Kilcullen Design
Cover Design: Marjory Dressler

Photo Credits: **p. 2:** Elizabeth Crews/Stock Boston; **p. 10:** Michael
Newman/Photo Edit; **p. 14:** Michelle Bridwell/Photo Edit; **p. 17:** Bob
Daemmrich/Stock Boston; **p. 18:** Richard Hutchings/Photo Edit;
p. 30: Bob Daemmrich/Stock Boston; **p. 38:** H. Gans/The Image Works;
p. 47: Mark Antman/The Image Works; **p. 48:** Bob Daemmrich/Stock
Boston; **p. 56:** Steve Ferry/P & F Communications; **p. 56:** Mary Kay
Denny/Photo Edit; **p. 71:** © Beryl Goldberg; **p. 72:** Spencer Grant/
Stock Boston; **p. 84:** © Beryl Goldberg; **p. 93:** © Beryl Goldberg;
p. 102: Skjold Photographs;

ISBN 0-8359-1843-2
Printed in the United States of America
9 10 11 12   06 05

Contents

UNIT 1

Recognizing Our Differences

Does this look like a typical class at your school? Maybe we would be better off if everyone looked alike. What if everyone thought alike, too? Maybe that would stop the prejudice, the conflict, and the differences of opinion we have to deal with every day.

But we don't all look alike or think alike. Life would be really boring if we did. Our differences, however, tend to cause tension and conflict because of the ways we respond to them.

This unit invites you to think about people's differences. The lessons and discussion questions will help you understand the many conflicts that can arise if we treat our differences as problems.

Different and Diverse!

Everyone was sitting in a circle. Mr. Hiro asked the class to count off. "To start this unit on conflict resolution, we're going to go around the circle and name ways in which we are the same and ways in which we are different.

"Each of you with an even number will tell us one way you are the same as the person to your right. Each with an odd number will tell us one way you are different from the person to your right."

Manuel had an even number. He glanced at Natalie, who was sitting to his right and staring at the floor. Natalie had just moved from Puerto Rico, where Manuel's grandparents still lived. *When it's my turn*, he wondered, *should I say that one way Natalie and I are the same is that our families come from the same country? Or should I just say we both have brown hair?*

Natalie, who had an odd number, peeked up at Kevin, sitting to her right. Kevin was the tallest person in the class. *Should I say we're different because he's tall and I'm short?* Natalie wondered. *Or should I pretend I don't notice and just say that my hair is brown and his is blond?*

Kevin had an even number. He thought about Jayne, who was to his right. He knew one way they were the same: they both had an alcoholic parent. They often saw each other at Alateen meetings. *Maybe I should just say we both have blond hair*, Kevin thought.

WHAT DO YOU THINK?

1. Do you think Manuel should tell the class that his family and Natalie's both come from Puerto Rico? Why or why not?

_____

_____

2. Should Kevin tell the class that he and Jayne both have an alcoholic parent? Why or why not?

_____

_____

3. Should all the students in this class just compare hair colors? Why or why not?

_____

_____

_____

Making Differences Work For You
● ●

Is the only similarity or difference among us the color of our hair? Of course not. We are the same and different in many ways, some visible and some invisible. Even twins who look exactly alike often have different skills, interests, values, opinions, and expectations.

Sometimes differences can lead to conflict. For example, let's say Eric and Stacey are working on the same science project, which is due tomorrow. There's lots of work left to do on this project. If the project is turned in late, their grade will go down. Stacey needs a good grade in science so she can stay on the swim team.

Eric is putting on his jacket and heading for the door. "I have to go," he tells Stacey. "I promised the coach I wouldn't miss another basketball practice." Both Eric and Stacey want to stay on their teams, but neither has told his or her thoughts to the other. They are headed for con-

A Closer Look

- The average 14-year-old boy is 5'2" tall, but common heights range from 4'10" to 5'10". (*World Almanac, 1995; Complete Home Medical Guide,* Crown, 1985)

- Alateen is a group for teenage children living in alcoholic families. Members usually meet once or twice a week to give support to each other and learn more about alcoholism.

flict. However, if Eric likes to draw and Stacey likes to write, these strengths can help them do a good job on this project.

If Stacey and Eric recognize and respect their differences, this project may be the best they've ever done. If they pretend they are the same, have the same skills, and want the same things, they may not be able to work together long enough to finish this project. (And one of them may be angry with the other for a long time.)

People *are* different—we look, think, and act differently.

Fitting In

Being part of a group—fitting in—can become really important at this stage in your life. Young people tend to dress alike, wear their hair alike, go to the same movies, and listen to the same music. This "alikeness" helps them feel that they fit in and are part of a group. Often, teenagers don't want anyone to think they are different in some way.

Maybe that's true of Natalie, who's new at school. As she looks around the class, it seems as if the other students have lived in this community all their lives. Being from Puerto Rico seems to mean being different, and right now that feels uncomfortable. Today, with Manuel's help, she may find out that many of the young people sitting in the circle are proud of their close ties to other cultures. She may find out that others also come from Puerto Rico.

Physical differences can seem important, when you're trying to fit in. But people don't pick their friends only by how they look. If we did, what might our friendships be like? Could you count on a friend just because he or she was tall or short?

Kevin knows he's taller than most kids his age, just like his dad. His father doesn't live at home anymore, but Kevin is glad that he looks more and more like his dad every day. He wouldn't mind if Natalie mentioned his height, as long as she didn't say something stupid about it.

But what about Jayne and the Alateen meetings? Should Kevin bring that up? Being open about similarities and differences doesn't mean blurting out personal information, especially about others. There's no reason for it in this situation. It would be better for Kevin to describe something else he and Jayne share: they both have little brothers who can be pests at times.

Keeping a Journal

Think of a person you consider to be a good friend of yours. In your journal, write one way the two of you are different. Then describe how this difference has led to a conflict, at least once.

Think of a specific person you barely know. In your journal, describe one way you and this person seem to be similar.

What About Conflict?

Think about the last time you had a disagreement with someone, at home or at school. Did you think, just for a minute, that you were right and the other person was wrong? Sometimes we forget that each of us is a unique individual, one of a kind. When we have different opinions, one person is not always wrong and the other person always right.

When we think of the other person as wrong, we are definitely headed for conflict. That can mean angry words, or even broken relationships we later regret.

Because we are all different, some conflict in our lives is unavoidable. It's a natural part of working together. Still, we can reduce the amount of conflict in our lives. We can also learn better ways to handle the conflicts we can't avoid.

One way to reduce our conflicts is to recognize how they can start. One way of starting a conflict is not respecting each other's differences. The more we respect each other, the better we can get along and work things out—instead of getting worked up!

TALK IT OVER

Form a circle with a group of six or more classmates, and do the exercise described at the beginning of this lesson. You might go around the circle to the right and then to the left. Discuss what you learn about each other.

THINK IT OVER

1. Describe a situation in which two people's differences could lead to conflict.

_____

_____

_____

2. Now describe a situation in which two people's differences could help instead of getting in the way.

_____

_____

_____

Sticks and Stones
and Stereotypes

Without reading further, see if you can match the people in the photo with the following professions: basketball player, scientist, teacher, physician, waiter/waitress.

How do you think you did? Would you be surprised to learn that Karl Walker, the man in the center, is finishing his residency in pediatrics at an Atlanta hospital? Masaji Suzuki, the second from the left, is the head waiter in his family's very popular Japanese restaurant.

On the left is Caroline Majors, the star player on her college basketball team. She now coaches the basketball team at her son's high school. John Foster, the second on the right, left his law practice last year. He is taking college courses so he can teach children, like his grandson, who are physically challenged. Rose Silva, on the right, just had her first scientific paper published. It was a study on Alzheimer's disease.

WHAT DO YOU THINK?

1. How many people in your class do you think could match the name tags correctly just by looking at the pictures? Why?

_____

_____

2. Since you probably don't know these people, how did you decide who should have each name tag?

_____

_____

3. Why do people often assume they know what someone is like, based on the way that person looks?

_____

_____

What's in a Label?

• •

Did you quickly match the basketball-player name tag with Karl Walker? If so, you may have been making decisions based on stereotypes. Stereotypes are a form of prejudice. They allow us to label others and to put them in categories.

When we use stereotypes, we make snap judgments about people. These judgments are based on the groups to which we think they belong. We may assume that we know what a person is like because of eye shape, age, or even skin color. We may put people in categories according to the kind of clothes they wear, or the neighborhoods where they live.

These kinds of assumptions can lead to misunderstandings and conflict. What if I think I can tell by looking at you how smart you are or what you're good at? I may be making some faulty assumptions. If I treat you in a certain way based on my faulty assumptions, we probably are going to have trouble working together.

Stereotypes keep us from really getting to know each other. Instead of jumping to conclusions based on how you look, I need to take time to get to know you as a unique individual. We are the same in some ways and different in other ways. If the only thing I notice is our differences, I may be missing an opportunity to gain a good friend.

PUTTING WORDS TO WORK

The words below are similar, but they do not mean the same thing.

- **Bias:** a preference for one thing over another, preventing fair judgment; prejudice.
- **Discrimination:** denying some people the rights or benefits that others have.
- **Prejudice:** liking or not liking someone or something without a good reason; prejudging people based on an assumption about the group to which they belong.
- **Racism:** believing that people of a certain race are inferior.
- **Stereotype:** a standard mental picture of a whole group of people; believing that everyone in a group is identical in certain ways.

Kinds of Stereotypes

You may be able to think of a number of stereotypes. For example, some people may believe that a certain group of people is lazy, while another group is too emotional. Some people may believe that all people in one group are intelligent. These stereotypes are inaccurate because they describe an entire group of people as if they were identical to each other.

For example, a teacher may become impatient with a Korean boy who is having trouble learning algebra. After all, "everyone knows" that math is easy for Asian people, so he must not be trying hard enough. A Chinese girl working on a group science project may resent being assigned to do the math computations. Perhaps she would rather make the presentation to the class.

All kinds of stereotypes keep us from getting to know each other as individuals.

Stereotypes Are Sneaky

Sometimes we don't even realize that prejudice and stereotypes are affecting our actions. Without thinking about it, we may avoid sitting next to certain people because of the way they are dressed. If we assume a girl does not speak English because of the shape of her eyes, we are prejudging her. If we expect a boy to be friendly (or hostile) because of the color of his skin, we are prejudging him.

Prejudice can cause conflict by encouraging us to listen carefully to some people, while ignoring others. Prejudice can also get in the way of resolving conflicts. This is especially true when we assume that we know how others feel and think.

Avoiding Prejudice and Stereotypes

Is your thinking clouded by prejudice or stereotypes? It may be if you:

- judge a whole group by the actions of one or two people,
- judge one person by the actions of anyone else,
- set low or high expectations based on a person's appearance,

Keeping a Journal

To identify some of your own positive or negative prejudices, in your journal, write the names of four groups of people, such as *New Yorkers, chess players, motorcycle riders,* and *actors.* Then add the word *all* to each group.

Beside each group, write the first three phrases you think of. Then review your phrases. They are good indications of your prejudices for or against the groups you listed.

Now answer this question in your journal: Do you personally know anyone in any of these groups? If not, why did you write those phrases?

- use words such as *all, none, every, always*, and *never* to describe an entire group of people. ("Those people *always* do that. They're *all* alike.")

TALK IT OVER

1. Choose a topic from the list below, and write a paragraph or two describing it. Try not to show any positive or negative feelings toward the topic. Then read your description aloud to a small group of classmates. Group members will try to detect bias (a positive or negative attitude) in your paragraph. After hearing each member's description, choose the most bias-free one to read to the class.

Nose rings	Brand-name sneakers
Curfews	Michael Jackson
R-rated movies	Allowances
Study hall	Professional baseball
Grateful Dead	Tattoos

2. In a small group, discuss some things a person might do to overcome a prejudice for or against a certain group of people. After five minutes of talking it over, select your two best ideas and share them with the class.

THINK IT OVER

1. Why might some people not be aware that they are prejudiced towards certain other people?

   _____

   _____

2. Why might an opinion about a person or group be prejudiced?

   _____

   _____

3. How can you make sure that your opinion about a person or group is not prejudiced?

   _____

   _____

Sources of Stereotypes

Is most prejudice and discrimination caused by the efforts of extremist groups, such as the Ku Klux Klan and skinheads? Unfortunately, no. If this were true, it would be easy to counteract the effects of these relatively small groups. Instead, prejudice, bias, and discrimination have many causes and many forms.

We learn some prejudice from our families, directly or indirectly. We are also exposed to our friends' biases. In addition, we get frequent lessons from television, newspapers, and movies about what certain groups are like and how they should be treated.

All this shapes our opinions and attitudes. Sometimes we end up with prejudices and stereotypes that are not only difficult to change, but even hard to identify. These attitudes can limit us. They can convince us that we must be friends only with people who are judged to be "acceptable."

These prejudices can also cause misunderstandings. They make it much harder to resolve the conflicts that occur as a normal part of living and working together.

WHAT DO YOU THINK?

1. What are some ways that families might unknowingly teach their children to be prejudiced?

_____

_____

2. How might your friends purposely or accidentally influence you to be prejudiced?

_____

_____

3. How do television and movies encourage prejudice?

_____

_____

Focus on Families
● ●

Children do learn prejudices from their families. These prejudices often are based on fear and misunderstanding. When members of a cultural group first arrive in an area, they usually have a different language and customs from most of the people living in that area. Unfortunately, people who are different are often seen as strange or even dangerous.

People already living here often worry that members of these new groups will take their jobs. These new people might not take care of their children or their houses in the same ways as the rest of us. They might even do better than people who have been living here for years.

It's easy to blame new groups for problems. A new group might be accused of causing an increase in crime or a loss of jobs. It's easy to attach negative labels to a new group. In this way, new prejudices are born.

Children absorb attitudes from their parents. And they always assume that their parents are right. Toddlers as young as three can begin to pick up prejudices. By the time they are four or five, they already know the "right" roles for males and females. They may not want to play with children of another race. They may feel uncomfortable around people who have physical limitations.

At twelve years of age, children who have been exposed to prejudice can already have firm stereotypes about cultural, racial, and religious groups.

MAKING A CONNECTION
TO SOCIAL STUDIES

Find out about the history of immigrant groups in your city or region. What were the first groups to settle there? Which groups followed them? Which groups are the most recent arrivals?

Which groups now live in your community? Which ones still tend to live together in their own neighborhoods?

This information might be available from your local chamber of commerce or at the library in local history books. Older people in the community might also be good sources of information.

Prejudice and Peers

As young people enter their teenage years, they naturally begin to separate from their families. They spend more time with their friends. If their friends happen to have the same prejudices as their parents, young people can conclude that *everybody* must think the same way.

The teenage years also tend to be a time when people are unsure of themselves. Occasionally, they can become a little overwhelmed by all the changes in their lives. Teenagers often try to impose some order to this confusion by setting "standards." These rules define how people should look and act. For example, everyone should wear a certain style and/or brand of clothes. Only certain hairstyles are "in."

The pressure from peers to fit into these "standards" can be strong. Some individuals—or even whole groups—put others down in order to make themselves feel more acceptable. It's easy to make fun of individuals or groups who look and act different. In this way, some young people gain new prejudices.

Stereotyping by the Media

Until recently, people from certain groups tended to be limited to certain roles in the movies and on television. Some were mostly shown as villains, criminals, and/or drug dealers. Others were generally shown as members of organized crime. Still others were portrayed as bloodthirsty savages.

People from these groups were rarely shown as human beings who share the same problems as most other Americans. Actors from various racial or cultural backgrounds have a much wider choice of roles now. Yet seeing stereotypes again and again in movies and on television has affected generations of Americans.

In recent years, the negative influence that television and radio talk shows have on public opinion seems to have increased. In order to boost their ratings, some talk shows discuss topics that stir up mistrust among a wide variety of groups. Many television talk shows encourage members of the audience to comment on others' lifestyles. Some radio talk shows invite listeners to call in and share their anger. Often, this anger is directed toward certain groups and is based on stereotypes.

Keeping a Journal

Over the next three days, keep a list of the stereotypes you encounter. They might include comments from friends or family, or stereotypes portrayed in movies, television shows, or commercials.

Also check your local newspaper. List the situations in which a person's race, cultural background, or occupation is identified.

Write a paragraph summarizing your findings.

Not a Joking Matter

• •

Have you ever heard or told a joke that made fun of a certain cultural group or the opposite sex? These jokes seem harmless—unless you are a member of the group being made fun of. Then they are annoying.

Cultural and gender jokes are based on stereotypes. They reinforce harmful misconceptions. People who laugh at these jokes seem to be agreeing with the stereotypes.

In order to treat people fairly and not be part of stereotyping, keep the following in mind:

- Think about what you say. Remember that jokes about certain groups can get a quick laugh, but cause lasting hurt.
- Speak up when someone tells a hurtful joke. You might simply say you don't think the joke is funny. Or ask the joke-teller to explain the joke. These kinds of jokes rarely make sense when someone tries to explain them.

TALK IT OVER

Work with four other students to think of ways in which television and movies stereotyped girls and women in the past. Share your conclusions with the class, along with specific examples. Then discuss the following questions as a class: Have these stereotypes changed? If so, in what ways? How could these stereotypes lead to conflict?

THINK IT OVER

1. Explain what you think this quotation means: "*We hate some people because we do not know them; and we will not know them because we hate them.*" Charles Caleb Colton, 1825.

_____

_____

2. Why do many people hesitate to speak up when someone tells a joke about another group?

_____

_____

"They're All Alike!"

WHAT DO YOU THINK?

1. Everyone in this picture belongs to the same ethnic group. What else makes them all the same?

   _____

   _____

2. Choose two people from this photo. Explain something that makes them each different from everyone else in the picture.

   Person #1

   _____

   _____

   _____

   Person #2

   _____

   _____

   _____

What About Conflict?

People are different—even people who look similar in some way. We have begun this book by discussing diversity and stereotypes because most conflict can be traced to these related sources:

- fear and misconceptions
- problems in communicating

It's easy to hate based on a stereotype. But once you get to know a person, it's almost always easy to find something to like.

TALK IT OVER

First impressions about people can be strongly influenced by stereotypes. Without mentioning any names, tell a group of classmates about a time when you overcame a negative first impression by getting to know someone. This person might be a friend, neighbor, teacher, coach, clerk at a store, or distant relative, for example. (Remember to show respect to the people in your group and in your class.)

THINK IT OVER

1. What are four ways in which racial or cultural groups can differ from each other?

   a. _____

   b. _____

   c. _____

   d. _____

2. What are four ways that people in the same racial or cultural group can be different from each other?

   a. _____

   b. _____

   c. _____

   d. _____

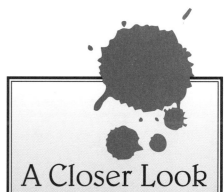

A Closer Look

As you read the achievements of the African Americans listed below, think about some of the stereotypes you have heard.

- **Maya Angelou:** distinguished poet
- **Benjamin Banneker:** inventor, astronomer, and mathematician who helped design and lay out Washington, D.C.
- **Ralph Bunche:** winner of the 1950 Nobel Peace Prize
- **Marian Wright Edelman:** founder of the Children's Defense Fund
- **Daniel Hale Williams:** surgeon who performed one of the first open-heart operations

(*World Almanac*, 1995)

Summing Up

- It is normal for people to have differences. Unless we recognize and accept them, differences can lead to conflict.

- Viewing people as stereotypes can keep us from getting to know them as real people.

- Prejudices and stereotypes are encouraged in many forms and by many influences in our lives.

- Two people from two cultural groups can be more similar than two people from the same cultural group.

Applying Ideas

1. For each statement below, explain what you think is the basis of the prejudice being shown.

   a. See that man driving that fancy car? How can he afford something that nice?

   _____

   _____

   _____

   b. Jason, go sit with Maria. She probably needs help with these math problems.

   _____

   _____

   _____

   c. The service here would be a lot better if they'd just hire some older workers.

   _____

   _____

   _____

   d. I won't give any more money to that homeless shelter downtown. One of those people spit on my shoe!

   _____

   _____

   _____

A Closer Look

Watch for these and other signs of positive and negative bias:

- judging a whole group by the actions of one or two people

- judging one person by the actions of anyone else

- setting low or high expectations based on someone's appearance

- using "loaded" words

- using generalizations to describe a group

- accepting someone's opinion without evaluating the source

Understanding Anger

Do some of the expressions on the faces below look familiar? Anger is as much a part of our lives as eating and sleeping. Yet, it may be our most misunderstood emotion.

People feel or don't feel angry for various reasons. But we still expect others to be angry when we are. We also expect them to be calm when we are. This kind of expectation can lead to conflict.

Anger can also cause conflict when our emotions get ahead of our thinking. Anger also can be the result of conflict. This happens when a simple disagreement heats up and turns into an argument.

Anger can cause many problems in relationships. Yet, few of us have tried to figure out why we get angry. Sometimes we don't realize that we *are* acting out of anger. We may not think about whether our way of responding will make the situation better or worse.

Our anger doesn't have to cause problems. It can help us get things done and make necessary changes. This unit will help you channel your own anger into inspiration—instead of into invitation to conflict and broken relationships.

Anger Provokers

"Keesha, you're 10 minutes late. We probably missed the best part of the movie. I told you to be here at 2:00!"

"Chill, would you, Amanda? We can stay and see the first part again. Anyway, you're not in charge of my life!"

Amanda (thinking): *I've been looking forward to seeing this movie all week. Keesha and I were going to be the first ones at school to see it. A ticket costs all the baby-sitting money I've saved, but I thought it'd be worth it. I even passed up a chance to go roller skating with my sister last night. I didn't have enough money for skating and for this movie.*

And now Keesha has made me miss part of it! I can't stay and see the first part again. It won't be on again till 5:30, and I have to be home by then. Keesha knows that! Why couldn't she be on time, just this once?

Keesha (thinking): *Finish your chores or no allowance, Mom kept saying. How was I to know they would take so long? And then I had to mop the kitchen floor on top of all the usual stuff I do! And after all that work and rushing around, this is the thanks I get! Who put Amanda in charge of the world? I'm sick of having people tell me what to do!*

WHAT DO YOU THINK?

1. Does Amanda have a right to be angry? Would you be angry if you were in her position? Why or why not?

_____

_____

_____

2. Does Keesha have a right to be angry? Would you be angry if you were in her position? Why or why not?

_____

_____

_____

Time for Anger?

• •

It's clear that different things provoke, or stir up, anger in different people. For example, last Friday night Erica, Aaron, Daryl, and Tamika went to their favorite pizza place. They had to wait a long time to be seated. Aaron, Daryl, and Tamika were so busy talking that they didn't notice the wait. Erica, however, got angrier and angrier. "They always serve adults first," she muttered. She folded her arms across her chest and glared at the waiters.

After the group was finally seated, Erica slowly relaxed and joined in on the conversation. Then a baby at the next table began crying. Erica, Aaron, and Tamika didn't seem to hear him, but Daryl rolled his eyes with each screech. "If that kid screams one more time...," he said through clenched teeth.

Daryl had spent too many hours listening to his baby sister cry at home. He surely didn't need to hear a baby screaming when he was out with his friends. He was angry because he thought the whole thing was unfair. Erica was angry because she thought the waiters didn't respect young people. Aaron and Tamika, on the other hand, were having fun—until it was time to go home.

On the way out of the crowded restaurant, Aaron bumped into a teenager he didn't know. The other boy called Aaron a name based on a group he thought Aaron belonged to. Aaron scowled all the way home, even though Daryl told him to forget about it. "He probably can't even spell that word," Daryl joked.

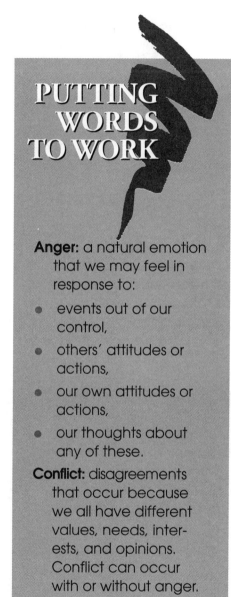

PUTTING WORDS TO WORK

Anger: a natural emotion that we may feel in response to:

- events out of our control,
- others' attitudes or actions,
- our own attitudes or actions,
- our thoughts about any of these.

Conflict: disagreements that occur because we all have different values, needs, interests, and opinions. Conflict can occur with or without anger.

19

Just as we have different skin colors and different goals, we feel angry over different things. Whether we become angry in a certain situation depends on many things. These things include our past experiences, our values, our self-confidence, and what we tell ourselves about the situation.

For example, if you tease me about my new haircut, I will smile. I know you are teasing me because you like me. If a stranger says the same thing, however, I may think he or she is putting me down. My reaction will be different, probably anger.

Anger is a normal emotion that occurs often during conflicts. What we do with our anger can either solve the conflict or turn it into a lasting problem.

Understanding the Causes of Anger

Stress is one major cause of anger. Stress is the pressure we feel in certain situations. Adrian is feeling stressed because she has an important report to finish tonight and a job to go to after school. As she hurries toward her locker after school, her friend Kelly stops her.

"Things are bad at home," Kelly says. "Do you have time to talk tonight?" What happens next surprises even Adrian. She snaps, "Can't you handle it yourself this time?" Adrian's stress has resulted in a kind of free-floating anger.

Frustration is similar to stress. We feel frustration when we can't reach goals that are important to us. Juan, for example, is determined to make the varsity football team this year. He's been eating right, working out with weights, and going to every practice. Now Coach Reynolds is posting the varsity team list on the bulletin board. The coach avoids looking at Juan. Juan knows then that his name isn't on the list.

Juan mutters, "Maybe the team wouldn't have such a lousy record if you picked some good players for a change!" The coach hears him and frowns. Juan's frustration has become anger. He has made a disappointing situation even worse.

Feeling *threatened* can also lead to anger, especially when the threat is to our self-esteem. Almost anything can be seen as a threat: a look, a shove, a put-down, a turned back, a phone call that isn't returned, not being waited on in a store. Any of these can communicate dis-

Keeping a Journal

Read the quotation below and explain what you think it means.

No man is angry that feels not himself hurt.
—Francis Bacon

Then describe two or three times when you felt hurt and became angry. Did any of these situations involve someone treating you like a stereotype because of your appearance or cultural background?

respect (or we may think they do). If we think others do not respect us, we often have angry feelings.

Being treated like a stereotype is another form of disrespect. Do you ever hear comments like the ones below? Whether the disrespect is intended or not, our anger level rises.

- "The music you kids listen to is disgusting."
- "Students with your background don't do well in college."
- "Girls aren't good at math."

Still, no one has to be at the mercy of anger. We can learn ways to control anger and make it work for us, not against us.

TALK IT OVER

Work in small groups to list three situations in which most people get angry. Now, share your list with the class. Note situations that were listed by several groups. Then discuss this question: Did your group easily agree on situations to include on your list? If not, why not?

THINK IT OVER

1. Is it okay to feel angry? Why or why not?

_____

_____

_____

_____

2. What are some problems that uncontrolled anger can cause?

_____

_____

_____

_____

Personal Peeves

Jarod is walking past a group of students. Some of them are his friends. As he walks past the group, they start laughing.

Are they laughing at me? They better not be. But why would they? Chip over there is on the soccer team with me. He's my friend. Wait—maybe he told them what happened at practice yesterday. No, he wouldn't do that. At least, I don't think he would.

But why are they laughing? Angelo is in my English class, and I had to give my report this morning. So I dropped all my note cards, but it wasn't that funny.

Maybe it's some kind of practical joke these kids pull on people who walk past them, just to see how they take it. I'm tough, but I don't like this at all.

Jarod is feeling pretty uncomfortable right now. He has a lot of mixed messages running through his head, most of them making him angry. He might be surprised to know that these young people are laughing at a joke one of the girls just told. No one in the group probably even noticed him.

WHAT DO YOU THINK?

1. Do you think Jarod should be worried about why the young people are laughing? Why or why not?

_____

_____

2. Would this situation cause you to become angry? If so, why?

_____

_____

Analyzing Anger

. . . .

Look over the list your group made at the end of Lesson 5, on page 21. You probably had no problems thinking of possible items for this list. There seem to be many situations in which we tend to become angry. You might have included people showing up late or "friends" ignoring you or people calling you names. Your list may have included being punished for someone else's mistake at school or at home. Or maybe you listed being cheated in a store.

Not all of the situations that your group listed might bother you personally. Yet, the first step in controlling our anger is recognizing the situations in which we do become angry. These situations are sometimes called "anger triggers." After we are aware of our anger triggers, we can think about the ways we respond to these situations. Are we making these situations better or worse?

To start analyzing your own anger triggers, fill in the survey of your "personal peeves" below.

Anger Triggers

. . . .

List four things that other people sometimes do or say that often cause you to become angry.

1. _____

2. _____

3. _____

4. _____

MAKING A CONNECTION

TO LANGUAGE ARTS

To find out more about the situations in which other people become angry, interview two people who are about your age (and who are not reading this book) and two people older than you (maybe family members or neighbors). Make up an interview form similar to the "Anger Triggers" survey, and record their answers.

Then write a one-page report that summarizes what you learned about anger from your interviews. Do not name the people you interviewed or share any information that might embarrass someone.

Now list four things that you do or say yourself that usually cause you, yourself to become angry.

1. _____

2. _____

3. _____

4. _____

Angry Messages

Many people probably do feel angry in the situations you listed in your survey. However, no person or situation can actually *make* anyone angry. We *can* make ourselves angry by what we tell ourselves about a situation. That's why some situations, such as waiting for a late friend, anger certain people but not others. (Remember Keesha and Amanda in Lesson 5?) What we tell ourselves about a situation allows us to shrug it off or encourages us to boil over.

Jarod could have asked the young people in the group what was so funny. He didn't because he was afraid they were laughing at him. Instead, he gave himself all kinds of negative messages about why they were laughing. By the time he had walked past, he was angry. Still, no one *made* him angry. He made himself angry.

When we talk about people or things that *make* us angry, we may feel helpless to control our anger. In reality, no one can make us angry without our help. And if we can avoid becoming angry, we are in a much better position to resolve those conflicts that are bound to come along.

TALK IT OVER

1. Talk over the situation below with your group.
   Situation: Latonya just found out that someone at school is telling everyone she shoplifted the new blouse she is wearing. Now she understands why some of her friends have been giving her strange looks.

   a. List something that Latonya could tell herself that would increase her anger.

   _____

   _____

b. What is something she might tell herself that would decrease her anger?

_____

_____

2. Now have everyone in the group write on an index card a situation in which young people tend to become angry. Don't sign the cards. Turn the cards over, and pick one to discuss. Think of one or two things that a person in that situation could think about that would increase his or her anger. Then identify one or two things that might decrease his or her anger. After discussing two or three of your cards, choose one and share your ideas with the class.

THINK IT OVER

1. How could you change how you respond to a situation that usually bothers you?

_____

_____

_____

2. Think about ways that your "anger triggers" have changed as you have gotten older.

   a. What is something that annoyed you in elementary school, but no longer bothers you?

_____

_____

   b. What is something that concerns and annoys you now, but did not when you were younger?

_____

_____

3. How can the negative messages that you give yourself about a situation lead to unnecessary conflict?

_____

_____

Keeping a Journal

Think of a time when you felt angry about a situation, but later learned that you misunderstood what was happening. An example would be Jarod becoming angry with his friends for "laughing at him."

Write a paragraph describing the situation and what you told yourself. Then think of a positive message that you will tell yourself if you're in a similar situation again.

Angles on Anger

"You just couldn't pass me the ball, could you, Gabe? You always have to be the star! It's your fault we lost the game."

Matt (thinking): *That Gabe! He never has been a team player, even in junior high. I was right under the basket! All he had to do was pass me the ball, but he takes the shot himself, as usual. And he missed! If it weren't for him, we'd be the city champs!*

Gabe (thinking): *Matt already forgot all the shots he missed during the game. I'll bet he blew at least six shots from the free-throw line. I'll be out of here in a minute, so I won't have to listen to him anymore. I just won't let him bother me.*

Matt and Gabe are both angry—at losing the game and perhaps at themselves. Yet each is handling his anger differently. Matt lets his out, way out. Gabe holds his in.

These are two examples of the ways we all deal with our anger. Did you realize that there are five main ways in which we respond to our anger? Learning more about them will help you analyze your own methods of coping with the strong, but unavoidable, emotion of anger.

WHAT DO YOU THINK?

1. Is Matt handling his anger in a positive way? Explain your answer.

_____

_____

2. Is Gabe handling his anger in a positive way? Explain your answer.

_____

_____

3. Which of the boys' responses to anger is more likely to lead to conflict? Why?

_____

_____

_____

Handling Anger

• •

What do you do when you're angry at a good friend? at a parent? at a teacher or coach? at a clerk in a store? In one situation, you might talk out your anger. In another, you might give the other person the silent treatment. In still another, you might pretend not to be angry. However, if you're like most people, you have a pattern to the way in which you express your anger. You tend to act the same way in similar situations, out of habit.

Responding out of habit is okay if we are responding constructively. However, some reactions, like Gabe's and Matt's, make a conflict worse instead of resolving it. Below are the most common patterns. Most people use different ones, in different situations. Some people use several of the responses in reacting to one problem or situation.

Denying Anger Some people, maybe some you know, refuse to admit they are angry. If they can't admit it to themselves, they can't admit it to others. Of course, this approach prevents them from resolving the conflict.

This bottled-up anger does not just disappear. It can lead to headaches, stomach aches, fatigue, and depression. Some people sleep, eat, or drink too much instead of admitting to themselves and others that they are angry. (Gabe is someone who denies his anger.)

MAKING A CONNECTION
TO SOCIAL STUDIES

How we deal with our anger is shaped by our cultural background. In some cultures, the expression of anger is not acceptable. In others, anger is expressed freely and often—then forgotten.

Talk with your family about the "anger rules" of your culture. (You may probably already know them!) Then write a one-page report describing these "rules." Remember that each person in a culture is an individual, not a stereotype. Do not write, for example, "Italians always..." or "Japanese never..."

MAKING A CONNECTION
TO ART

What does anger look like to you? Is it explosive—or hidden and controlled? In an art medium of your choice, show how you think it looks. The medium might be watercolors, torn paper, a collage, charcoal, a videotape, or any other form that is available to you.

If you wish, share your work with the class.

Turning Anger Inward Some people admit they are angry, but they turn their anger against themselves. They believe they are at fault in most conflicts. They should have worked harder, known better, planned ahead, stayed home, not mentioned a certain subject, and so on. Blaming themselves can become a habit. They may begin to believe that they cannot do anything right.

Turning anger inward can lead to depression. Because depressed people blame themselves for any conflicts that occur, they tend to withdraw from contact with others. They can become seriously ill unless they receive help with their feelings.

Avoiding Anger Other people admit to themselves that they're angry, but they are very uncomfortable dealing directly with conflict. They might change the subject or leave the room. They might also express their anger to people not involved in the conflict. They may gossip or complain about the "offender."

Avoiders may insist to the people directly involved that they are not angry. ("Angry, me? Of course not. Why would I be angry?") Instead, they act out their feelings. For example, they may slam doors, avoid chores, show up late, or get poor grades.

Not dealing with a conflict can also be a way of controlling a relationship. The avoider has the power to decide when and if the conflict will be discussed and resolved. The other person is powerless. Avoiders may hold grudges based on misconceptions and misunderstandings. Since they will not admit there is a problem, a hurtful situation cannot be cleared up.

Blaming Others Another method of dealing with conflicts is to blame others for the problem, as Matt did. Blamers think they have a right to be angry because others are always at fault. They tend to express their anger loudly and freely. This free expression often leads others to react with their own free expression—or to leave the situation. In either case, the conflict is unresolved.

Tackling the Problem To tackle the problem, we recognize that we are angry, identify the reason for our anger, and try to change whatever is wrong. For example, we might study differently to get a better grade on the next test, check with a friend before changing plans we made together, or promise not to be late next time. Now we have responded to our anger by trying to resolve the conflict.

TALK IT OVER

1. Discuss this question with your group: Why do we tend to handle our anger differently in different situations? After about ten minutes of exploring this topic, share one or two of your conclusions with the class.

2. Think about the situation below, and write how someone might react in each style of managing anger. *Situation:* Last week, Philip, your best friend, borrowed your newest CD. You ask for it back, and he says he loaned it to Gerald. You never would have loaned it to Gerald, who always loses things. Now Gerald can't find your CD.

   a. Denying Anger: _____

   _____

   b. Turning Anger Inward: _____

   _____

   c. Avoiding Anger: _____

   _____

   d. Blaming Others: _____

   _____

   e. Tackling the Problem: _____

   _____

THINK IT OVER

1. Is it possible to avoid feeling angry? Why or why not?

   _____

   _____

2. Wouldn't the world be more pleasant if no one expressed angry feelings? Why or why not?

   _____

   _____

3. What can happen if we don't separate angry feelings from angry actions?

   _____

   _____

Angry? Me?

Each of these girls is angry, but notice the different ways that they cope with this uncomfortable feeling. How do you deal with your own anger? Fill in the survey below to start analyzing your reactions to anger.

Anger Inventory

Write O (often), S (sometimes), or N (never) beside each action to show how often you respond that way when you are angry. This is a personal survey that you will not be asked to share.

When I am angry, I...

_____ **1.** think the problem is my fault.

_____ **2.** take a nap or have a snack.

_____ **3.** stay away from the other person, but tell friends how much he or she annoyed me.

_____ **4.** take my anger out on another friend or on my younger brother or sister.

_____ **5.** tell the person specifically what he or she did wrong.

_____ 6. realize that my anger might make it hard for me to think clearly.

_____ 7. remind the person of all the times and ways that he or she has annoyed me lately.

_____ 8. wish I had done things differently.

_____ 9. think of ways to avoid the problem next time.

_____ 10. wonder why the other person can never do anything right.

TALK IT OVER

1. Without revealing how you filled in your own survey, work in a group to put each action listed in the survey into one of these categories. Write the number of each action on one of the lines below.

   Denying Anger: _____

   Turning Anger Inward: _____

   Avoiding Anger: _____

   Blaming Others: _____

   Tackling the Problem: _____

   Group members might disagree about the category for an action because they interpret the action differently. Even so, talking the actions over will help you analyze your own responses to anger.

2. Discuss this question with your group: Why is it difficult to have a friend who denies it when he or she is angry? What about a friend who avoids dealing with anger?

THINK IT OVER

1. Compare the categories of responses above with how you filled in your personal inventory. What surprises you about the pattern you see?

   _____

   _____

2. How can the results of your inventory help you handle anger?

   _____

   _____

Keeping a Journal

Think about a recent time when you felt angry. Describe the situation and how you dealt with your anger. Then explain whether your response improved the situation.

Now describe two other responses that you could have used in the same situation. Explain whether each one would have been more helpful or more harmful than what you actually did.

Keeping a Journal

Think about your usual responses to anger. Which one seems to cause you the most problems? Leaving the room when someone disagrees with you? Not admitting when you are angry? Blaming yourself too often? Blaming others too often?

Prepare a one-week plan for working on this problem. For example, you might talk over the situation with a parent or friend on the first day. On the second day, you might record every time you are tempted to respond to anger in this way.

Try out your plan, and see if you can begin to change the way you respond to your anger.

Summing Up

- People feel or don't feel angry about various things.
- Thinking about what makes us angry is the first step in controlling our anger and avoiding unnecessary conflicts.
- People respond to their anger in various ways.
- Analyzing the ways in which we respond to our anger helps us choose more constructive responses.

Applying Ideas

Identify the kind of response to anger in each description below. Write one letter beside each statement.

a. Denying Anger   **d.** Turning Anger Inward

b. Avoiding Anger   **e.** Blaming Others

c. Tackling the Problem

_____ 1. After Heather lost Lamar's sweater, she started walking to school instead of riding the bus that he rides.

_____ 2. Kevin keeps saying that if Patrick were off the team, they'd win more games.

_____ 3. Monisha made an appointment with her language arts teacher to get some extra help with an essay.

_____ 4. Shaun decided not to try out for the team again because he probably wouldn't make it.

_____ 5. Karl's mother has gained 15 pounds since she had to go back to work.

_____ 6. Tabitha told her little brother that she was sorry she had yelled at him. She said she was feeling angry because of something that had happened at school.

_____ 7. William told Tiffany that he didn't mind if she went to the movies with Veronica, but then he didn't come to her birthday party the next day.

_____ 8. Yvonne's boyfriend broke up with her, but she can't figure out what she did wrong.

UNIT **3**

Dealing With Your Anger

What happens when anger slips out of control? Have you ever been angry and said or done something that you regretted later? Most people have. If you wish you could take back even one angry word or act, you already know why it's important to control your anger.

Babies express their anger in tears and cries. When adults shout and throw things, though, they're regarded as immature, bossy, self-centered, demanding, or dangerous.

Think about people you know who can't or don't control their anger. How do you react when they start acting out their angry feelings instead of handling them? Many people leave the situation if they can. They may also stand there, quietly building up their own angry feelings. If you happen to be the target of such a person's anger, you may feel like attacking back.

Even after you've identified the situations and the people that you are likely to make you angry (as you did in Unit 2), you can't always avoid them. You can, however, realize when you are becoming angry and take steps to handle that anger—before it gets the best of you.

Recognizing When You're Angry

Is anger all in your mind? It certainly starts there, but it soon spreads throughout your body. The anger you feel in your brain sends physical signals to all parts of your body. These signals let your heart, your muscles, and the rest of your body know that something is not right in your world.

How does this feel? You already know. Whether it's a headache, stiff shoulders, a burning face, or that hot "acidy" feeling in your stomach, you have certainly felt symptoms of anger. However, in the heat of the moment, you may not always recognize these symptoms. You may be so focused on what someone else is doing or saying that you miss what's happening within your own body.

If you don't realize you're getting angry, how can you do something constructive about it? Angry feelings are easier to control when they start to build—before they gain so much strength that they begin to take over your actions. This lesson will help you notice those angry feelings coming before they sneak up and overpower you.

WHAT DO YOU THINK?

1. Use the numbers in the diagram to identify the people you think are angry. Explain how you know.

_____

_____

_____

2. Why do you think that some of the young people in the picture do not seem to be angry?

_____

_____

3. Do you think that the angry people in the picture realize that they are visibly angry? Would it help them to know that?

_____

_____

The Body's Reaction to Anger

• •

To better understand how your body handles anger, consider how animals respond to danger. A robin who sees a cat approaching will usually fly away. However, a parent robin protecting its nest may stay and fight. In both cases, as soon as the bird is aware of the danger, its body provides the extra energy that it will need to fight or flee.

Long ago, humans faced mostly physical danger. This same fight-or-flight response gave people the energy they needed to survive. Now, however, this type of danger is rare. Much of the danger you face today is emotional. You are threatened more often by others' words than by their actions. You usually neither fight nor flee in these situations. Yet, your body still prepares for action.

When you feel threatened, your *adrenal glands* pump a hormone called *adrenaline* into your bloodstream. Adrenaline increases the level of sugar in your blood, giving you more energy. In a true emergency, this extra energy has allowed people to lift cars to rescue people who were trapped underneath. However, when you're merely angry, all this extra energy isn't so helpful.

PUTTING WORDS TO WORK

- **Adrenal glands:** two glands, located near the kidneys, that help the body respond to anger or stress; they also have other functions.

- **Adrenaline:** a hormone released by the adrenal glands

- **Hormones:** chemical messengers produced by glands and circulated in the bloodstream; hormones control many body functions.

- **Sympathetic nervous system (SNS):** the part of the nervous system that controls smooth muscles, such as those in the digestive system, and blood vessels

At the same time, the body's *sympathetic nervous system* (SNS) helps prepare you for action. This system slows down body functions that aren't needed in an emergency, such as digestion. At the same time, it speeds up other body functions, as shown in the diagram below.

Unfortunately, adrenaline keeps pouring into your bloodstream during the whole time you are angry. This extra stimulation to your body systems can harm your health if it continues too long. It is especially stressful to the heart and circulatory system and can contribute to high blood pressure.

Anger Attack

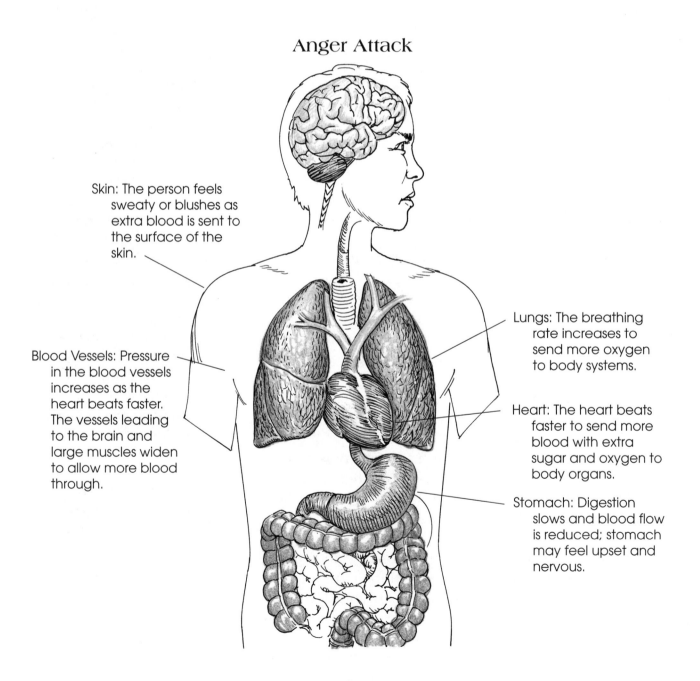

Skin: The person feels sweaty or blushes as extra blood is sent to the surface of the skin.

Blood Vessels: Pressure in the blood vessels increases as the heart beats faster. The vessels leading to the brain and large muscles widen to allow more blood through.

Lungs: The breathing rate increases to send more oxygen to body systems.

Heart: The heart beats faster to send more blood with extra sugar and oxygen to body organs.

Stomach: Digestion slows and blood flow is reduced; stomach may feel upset and nervous.

Beyond Your Body

Is your body's response to anger just a problem for your heart and blood vessels? Unfortunately, no. The tension you feel from this fight-or-flight response can push you into action. You might shout, wave your arms, run, cry, scream, pound the wall—or hit someone. You usually don't plan these actions. You may not even realize that you're doing them. Your body is just trying to use up the extra energy flowing through your bloodstream.

Of course, these actions usually do little to solve the problem. Instead, you need to recognize the tension you feel and learn positive ways to relieve it. (You'll learn more about taking positive actions in the next lesson!)

TALK IT OVER

In a small group, discuss the large and small signs that let you know that you're getting angry. These might range from a tight feeling in your shoulders, to a faster breathing rate, to clenched fists. Identify three or four symptoms that most group members have felt at some point. Share your list with the class.

THINK IT OVER

1. Do you always realize when you're getting angry? Why or why not?

_____

_____

_____

2. Is it better if you don't dwell on your angry feelings? Why not just ignore them?

_____

_____

3. How can other people tell you're angry, even if you don't realize it?

_____

_____

Keeping a Journal

Choose two symptoms of anger that you often experience. Keep a record for two days of each time you feel either symptom. Write what was happening or what you were thinking at that time.

At the end of two days, read your notes. Write a paragraph explaining what you learned about your responses to anger.

Playing It Cool

I can't believe it! Rory said he was going to the library, Angela thought. *What is he doing talking to Cathy?*

Angela is dangerously close to losing control of her anger. What can happen when angry feelings grow until they get out of control? Part of the answer can be found every evening on the 6:00 news. The newspaper, too, is full of stories about shootings, beatings, and small children who are rushed to the emergency room after "falling down the stairs." Many of these deaths and injuries were caused by anger that had built up until someone exploded in fury.

The availability of guns has greatly increased the damage caused by out-of-control anger. Ten years ago, an argument over a quarter might have resulted in name-calling or maybe a black eye. Recently, it led to the death of a 12-year-old in Chicago. The killer, who was only 16 himself, believed that the younger boy was being disrespectful. Not knowing how else to handle his anger, the teenager shot the boy.

The most frequent results of angry outbursts aren't reported on the news. These include broken friendships and

hurt feelings. How often have you heard someone say, "I was so mad I...." Whatever action comes next in this sentence, it usually made the situation worse instead of better.

This lesson will help you cool down those angry feelings so that you can think clearly. That way, you'll be less likely to do or say something that you'll regret later.

WHAT DO YOU THINK?

In the above situation, Angela's anger may be keeping her from thinking clearly. What are some possible explanations for this situation that she should consider?

_____

_____

Taking Inventory

• •

You might be out with friends, eating dinner with your family, or sitting alone doing homework. Suddenly, you realize that your heart is pounding and your jaw is clenched. Your body is full of energy with no place to go. What's happening?

First, take an inventory of how you're feeling. Ask yourself:

- Am I under stress? If so, what kind?
- Do I feel frustrated? If so, why?
- Do I feel threatened or rejected? If so, by whom?
- Does something seem unfair? If so, what?

If the answer to any of these questions is "yes," your physical symptoms are probably signs of building anger. These questions may help you figure out what's bothering you. However, before you do anything else, you need to cool down. No one thinks clearly when his or her fists are clenched.

The information in the left-hand column of the chart on the next page offers suggestions for what to do when you are angry and need to cool down in a hurry. The right-hand column suggests ways to work on those angry feelings when you have more time. You may have heard several of these ideas before, but sometimes the best advice is old advice. There are no magical ways to control your anger. You just have to find the techniques that work for you.

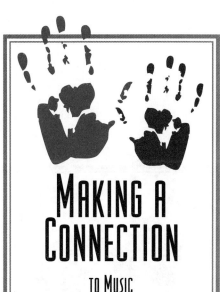

MAKING A CONNECTION

TO MUSIC

What kinds of music do you find relaxing? a soft instrumental? a country-western ballad sung by someone who has the same problems as you do? a hard-rock favorite that's so loud that you can't hear your angry thoughts?

Choose a song that you think is especially relaxing. Then write a paragraph in your journal explaining what you like about it. You might also play it for a small group or for the class. (If necessary, you might be able to borrow a recording from the library.)

When You're Really Angry	When the Crisis Is Past— But You're Still Angry
• Count to 10, or 100, if necessary.	• Use up that extra adrenaline by working out or playing a sport. Do some jumping jacks, or pound a pillow!
• Take a deep breath. Breathe in deeply through your nose, and breathe out slowly through your mouth. Repeat several times.	• Try some relaxation techniques. For example, start at your toes, and contract and relax each group of muscles. As you slowly work toward your head, think calm thoughts.
• Unclench your fists, and relax your shoulder muscles.	• Listen to your favorite music.
• Tell the other person that you need time to calm down so that you won't say or do something you might regret later. If necessary, set a time to talk about this conflict again.	• Take a walk, or read a book.
• Ask yourself if this problem is going to seem important next week or in two years? (Try to put the situation into perspective.)	• Talk over the problem with a person that you trust and who is not involved.
• Remind yourself that you've handled bigger problems than this. If necessary, think of someone you can ask for advice.	• Help someone else. Cook something to surprise your family, or help your little brother with his homework.
	• Write a poem or song explaining how you feel.

Wrong!

Some young people, and some adults, think that smoking cigarettes helps a person calm down. However, cigarettes and other tobacco products contain the drug *nicotine.* Nicotine is a stimulant that speeds up bodily functions, including the heartbeat. People who are addicted to nicotine feel shaky when they don't get enough of this drug. Smoking more nicotine will usually get rid of this shakiness. Nevertheless, feeding an addiction is not the same as calming down when you're angry.

MAKING A CONNECTION

TO LANGUAGE ARTS

Create a bulletin board of recent newspaper and magazine articles that show the results of uncontrolled anger.

When the board is full, select several of the more detailed articles. Form groups. Give one to each group. The members of each group will read their article and try to determine the cause(s) of the person's anger. Suggest better ways to handle the situation and the anger.

Other young people, and some adults, believe that drinking calms a person down. Alcohol is a depressant that slows the brain, causing people to feel sleepy. However, alcohol also affects people's judgment; drinkers tend to do and say things that they wouldn't do or say if they hadn't been drinking. In addition, drinking can cause a person's mood to intensify. Thus, a sad person becomes sadder—and an angry person becomes angrier and less in control.

TALK IT OVER

Sit with a group of classmates, and talk about ways that you calm down when you're angry. Choose two or three that you think work best, and have a group reporter share them with the class. Compile a class list on posterboard. Keep the list posted to remind everyone of good ways to handle anger.

THINK IT OVER

1. Some people think that it's a good idea to get rid of angry feelings by telling the other person exactly what they think of him or her. Is this a good idea? Why or why not?

_____

_____

_____

2. Why is vigorous physical activity a good idea when you're angry?

_____

_____

_____

3. How do you know that your thoughts can start adrenaline flowing?

_____

_____

_____

Sending Yourself the Right Messages

• Mrs. Ortega has never liked me.	• I didn't understand this topic very well. I'll do better next time.
• She only gives good grades to kids who raise their hands all the time.	• I'll ask Mrs. Ortega to look at my rough draft next time, as she offered.
• This topic was way too hard to write about.	
	• My parents know how hard I worked on this—they'll understand.
• I'll bet this is the worst grade in the class.	• Now I see what I did wrong. Maybe Mrs. Ortega will let me rewrite this.
• My parents are going to hit the roof when they see this!	• She did like my title.

We spend much of the day talking to ourselves. Some of the time we comment on other people. ("He smiled at me! Maybe he's thinking about asking me to the dance!") But much of the time we focus on ourselves, constantly rating how we're doing. We may give ourselves pats on the back. ("That's two baskets in a row!") Or we may point out real or imagined failures. ("Why can't you remember which keys print the page?")

Using these messages, we can be our own cheerleaders—or our own worst enemies. Our messages to ourselves can lead us into or out of conflict. To make sure that such messages are helping and not hurting, we need to listen carefully to what we're telling ourselves.

WHAT DO YOU THINK?

1. How could the thoughts in the left-hand column of the chart on page 42 lead a person into conflict?

_____

_____

2. How could the thoughts in the right-hand column of that chart help a person to avoid conflict?

_____

_____

Thinking in the Rain
• •

It's not easy to think positive thoughts when we're angry. Whether we're mad at others or mad at ourselves, the first thing we tend to look for is someone to blame. So we put others down, or we put ourselves down. We go on to imagine the worst possible consequences of the situation. Then we think about who's to blame again. "How could he/she/I do this! I'll never be able to look anyone in the face again!"

With all these negative thoughts, it's no wonder we get angrier. Our muscles get tighter, our stomachs churn, and our hearts start racing.

Thinking these kinds of thoughts in response to anger can become a habit. We don't consider whether these messages to ourselves make sense. We just play the same old tapes in our heads, over and over.

So what can we do instead? It seems too simple to say "Think positive thoughts." Yet, with some practice, most of us can get out from under that dark cloud that rushes over our heads at the first sign of a problem. It is possible to break our old habits. We can train ourselves to stand in the sunshine instead of raging in the rain. The first step is to listen to that little voice in our heads. We need to analyze what we're telling ourselves. Then we'll be ready to make some changes, if we need to.

Keeping a Journal

The very next time you feel your anger rising, listen—really listen—to what you're telling yourself about the situation. Write your thoughts in your journal or on a piece of paper.

After you are calm again, read the thoughts that you jotted down. Were you thinking of ways to solve the problem—or were you choosing someone, such as yourself, to blame? What effect did your thoughts have on your attitude?

Now write a positive thought about the situation for each negative one that you listed.

Problem	Thoughts encouraging anger	Thoughts encouraging calmness
Someone at school is gossiping about you.	Everyone's against me! They all hate me!	My friends know that gossip is false.
You have the earliest curfew of any of your friends.	When are my folks going to stop treating me like a baby!	My parents are worried about what might happen to me. I'll have to reassure them that I won't take chances with my safety.
Your best friend told someone a secret that you didn't want anyone to know.	Some friend! I will never trust her again in my life!	Maybe I didn't tell her that it was a secret. I'll ask her why she did it.

Keeping a Journal

Look back at your own anger triggers from Lesson 6. Read your list of things that other people say or do that make you angry. For each one, write what you usually tell yourself about the situation.

Now read your list of things you say or do that result in your becoming angry. For each one, write the message you give yourself in that situation. Then read over your messages to yourself, and explain what you learned about your anger.

Seeking Serenity

Anger can be helpful when it causes us to make a needed change. You might feel angry about a low grade and promise yourself to study harder or differently the next time. That's an example of using anger constructively. But what if you're angry because you're too short to be a professional basketball player or a model? In this case, anger will only make you more unhappy.

One key to mental health is to recognize which situations you can change and which you cannot change, no matter how angry you are. Some teenagers, for example, feel extremely angry because a parent is an alcoholic. These teens tend to pour on the guilt and pour out the bottles. Yet, they are trying to change a situation over which they have little control. Instead, they can change the only person who is under their control—themselves. They might talk with a counselor or attend Alateen meetings. Both of these actions are much more helpful than huddling under that dark, angry cloud.

Think about times when you feel angry about a situation that you can't control. It might involve a storm that cancels a baseball game or a friend who likes someone else now. This anger is wasted! Save it for times when you could use that extra energy.

44

Do you ever feel angry because others do things differently than you do? Maybe one friend thinks about something forever and asks a million questions before making up his mind. Another friend decides quickly, but changes her mind at the last minute, after you've made all the plans. One or both of these behaviors could drive you crazy, but only if you let them. Do you really want everyone to do things exactly the way you do them? What a boring world that would be!

TALK IT OVER

In groups of four, will make up a chart with the same three headings as in the chart on page 44. Then, with group members sitting in a circle, one person will write a problem under the first heading and read it to the group. The next person to the right in the circle will write a negative thought under the second heading and read it aloud. The next person will write a positive thought under the third heading and read it.

Finish at least three problems. Then choose one problem and share it and both related thoughts with the class.

THINK IT OVER

1. Why do you think people tend to think negative thoughts about a situation instead of positive ones?

   _____

   _____

2. Practice thinking positively by finishing these sentences:

   a. Jenna got the role I wanted in the play, but

   _____

   b. Karl called me a name in the locker room, but

   _____

   c. I have detention for something I didn't do, but

   _____

   d. The coach cut me from the team for missing practices, but

   _____

Summing Up

- If we recognize the physical symptoms of anger, we will be more aware of our anger and better able to control it.
- We need to learn ways to calm down so that we can think about a problem clearly and not make it worse.
- What we tell ourselves about a problem or conflict strongly influences whether we feel angry.

Applying Ideas

For each of the situations below, explain the technique that you could use to calm down. (Don't repeat any.) Then write a negative message and a positive message about the situation.

Situation A: You need a good grade on the math final to get into Algebra 2 next year. That's why you've been studying so hard. During the test, the guy who sits behind you, whispers, "Move over so I can see your answers." The teacher hears the whispering and gives you both an F on the test.

A way you could calm down:

_____

A negative message to yourself: _____

_____

A positive message to yourself: _____

_____

Situation B: You walk over to the lunch table where you usually sit with your friends, but Shayna is sitting in your seat. "Shayna," you say, "that's my seat." She smiles up at you. "Oh, really? Well, I'm sitting here today."

A way you could calm down:

_____

A negative message to yourself: _____

_____

A positive message to yourself: _____

_____

UNIT 4

Communicating to Avoid Conflict

"Alicia, I told you a hundred times already—that won't work," said Kyle impatiently.

Alicia (thinking): *Kyle thinks he knows everything! If he would just stop talking for a minute, I could explain what I really meant. His idea isn't any better than mine, but I may never get a chance to say what my idea is!*

Kyle (thinking): *Does Alicia always talk so slowly? I've only got 20 minutes before I have to leave for my after-school job. If we don't hurry up and make some decisions, we'll never get this done.*

When Alicia and Kyle were assigned to do this project together, they didn't know each other well. At this rate, they are not going to get to know each other any better. They are so annoyed with one another that they are not really communicating. If they can't work together, how are they going to do a good job on this project?

What is keeping these two people from exchanging the information that would help them plan this project? Unit 4 will help you pinpoint the things that help—and don't help—people communicate with one another.

Not Listening Leads to Conflict

"I think I have a good chance to make the team," Justin said, "if I can just get more strength in my swing."

"Don't worry about your swing, Justin," Rose told him. "You just need to eat right. I take vitamins every day."

"The coach showed me some exercises that are already ..."

"I exercise, too!" she said. "I have a videotape of aerobics that I do almost every morning. It's a tough workout!"

"These exercises use free weights and ..."

Rose laughed and patted her stomach. "Hey, I have some free weight you could have if you want it!"

Justin stared at her for a second, shook his head, stood up, and walked away. *What did I say?* Rose wondered. *We were just talking about exercises.*

Rose and Justin were both talking, but were they communicating? The next time Justin has something he's concerned about, he might look for someone who is a better listener.

Like Justin, we can usually tell when people are too busy with their own interests and thoughts to pay attention to what we have to say. We often see their lack of attention as a lack of respect. This lack of respect, whether it was intended or not, can get in the way of friendships. That's what happened with Rose and Justin.

This lesson will help you become more aware of behaviors that can get in the way of good listening. That way, you can avoid poor listening—and some unneeded conflict in your life.

WHAT DO YOU THINK?

Are Rose and Justin communicating? Why or why not?

_____

_____

This Way to Conflict
• •

How can you tell whether another person is listening to you? How do you feel when that person is not listening?

Most people would like to shout "You're not listening to me!" at least a couple of times a week. Instead, they swallow their anger. They might also start disagreeing with the other person over little things. In any case, not listening can get in the way of relationships and lead to conflict.

Three of the main verbal ways that people show they are not listening are interrupting, telling your own story, and giving advice. (The nonverbal ways in which people show they are not listening are discussed in Lesson 14.)

Interrupting Interrupting can sometimes lead to a conflict. For example:

Karen: My mom and I had a big fight before I left for school this morning and …

Keisha: Was it over your sweater again?

Karen: No, it was my brother. He …

Keisha: Is he still trying to get you to do his homework?

Karen: No, he wants my mom to …

Keisha: Wait—let me guess: He wants her to get another dog, right?

Karen: No! Keisha! Would you just let me finish?

PUTTING WORDS TO WORK

- **Hearing:** detecting sound waves
- **Listening:** using techniques that help you understand what the other person is saying
- **Talking:** saying words
- **Communicating:** exchanging knowledge and information
- **Nonverbal:** without using words
- **Verbal:** using words

How do you react when other people finish your sentences for you? And what about when they start their own sentences—in the middle of yours? Keisha's interruptions are greatly increasing the frustration that Karen already feels because of whatever happened to her at home that morning.

Telling Your Own Story Sometimes telling your own story can lead to a conflict. For example:

Alfred: Wait till I tell you what happened yesterday! Jeremy and I went to the ballpark, and who do you think we saw? Cal Ripken!

Ahmad: Oh, yeah? Well, once my uncle took me to a Chicago Bulls' game, and I saw Michael Jordan!

Alfred: Cal wasn't even playing. He was just there to watch the game, I guess. He looked great!

Ahmad: Michael walked right by where we were sitting. I think he looked at me! I bought a poster of him and put it in my bedroom.

Alfred: Well, Jeremy and I were excited, anyway.

Do you know people who seem to be listening, but they're really just waiting for you to stop talking? Then they jump in with their own story. And what happened to them is always better—or worse—than what happened to you. How do you feel then?

Giving Advice Giving un-asked for advice also can lead to conflict. For example:

April: I just got this CD by Whitney Houston from that record club, but I'm not sure I like it.

Audrey: You shouldn't even belong to that club. Why don't you join the club I belong to? They have much better deals.

April: I like the rest of Whitney's CDs, but this one is different. It's more, you know, country-western.

Audrey: Country-western? That's out now! I'll give you a list of the CDs everyone likes. You can listen to those.

April didn't ask for advice about which record club she should belong to or which CDs she should listen to. Audrey told her these things anyway. Do you have friends who always know a better way to do something than the way you did it? Their unasked-for advice surely discourages conversation.

All three of these poor listening habits interfere with communication. That often means conflict. The best way to handle conflict is to avoid it in the first place. The next lesson describes ways to be a better listener so you can avoid at least some of the conflict in your life!

Keeping a Journal

Think about your own listening habits. Do you get so eager in conversations that you interrupt others? Do other people's stories remind you of times when similar things happened to you? Can you always think of a bit of advice that could help someone?

Identifying a problem is the first step in doing something about it. You've already taken the first step!

TALK IT OVER

1. Work with a group of three other students to list three or four other behaviors that make you think that the other person is not listening. (Do not mention anyone by name.) Save these group lists to review after Lesson 14, on nonverbal listening, and after Lesson 15, on listening in various cultures.

2. Each group will write a dialogue that has one character who is not listening. Read your dialogue aloud within your group to make sure that it sounds like a real conversation. Then read your dialogue to the class. After each dialogue is read, discuss what the nonlistener said or did to show that he or she was not listening. Then explore how someone might feel if he or she were not being listened to in this conversation.

THINK IT OVER

1. Why is careful listening a sign of respect?

   _____

   _____

2. Think of someone who is a good listener. (This time you can name the person.) Write at least three things that make this person a good listener.

   a. _____

   b. _____

   c. _____

3. Look back over the anger triggers that you listed on page 24. In the space below, write any triggers that relate to someone not listening to you.

   _____

   _____

4. What is a positive message you can give yourself if you think that someone is not listening to you?

   _____

   _____

Listening That Avoids Conflict

Veronica: Is your sister going to try out for the play? If she does, I don't have a chance of getting the lead role!

Patrick: I don't know. Ebony doesn't tell me much anymore.

Veronica: She doesn't talk to you?

Patrick: Not much. I've been kind of worried about her, ever since she started hanging out with Beneka. I mean, Ebony and Beneka take off for hours every night. I wonder where they go.

Veronica: Do you think they might be into something?

Patrick: Yeah, maybe.

Veronica: Does your dad notice what's happening?

Patrick: I'm not sure. I guess I should ask him, huh? I think I will. Thanks, Roni. I've got a plan now.

Are Patrick and Veronica communicating? Yes! They are not only exchanging information, but Veronica is also listening for the feelings behind Patrick's words.

She is giving him an opportunity to share his concerns with her, if he wants to.

Are Patrick and Veronica headed for conflict? Probably not. This lesson will help you avoid conflict as you learn approaches to better listening—and it will help you learn to solve problems instead of creating them.

WHAT DO YOU THINK?

1. How does Veronica encourage Patrick to talk to her?

She does _____

_____

She does not _____

_____

2. How might the conversation have been different if Veronica had said, "Oh, sisters are like that!" instead of "She doesn't talk to you?"

_____

_____

A Priceless Gift

Listening, really listening, is a precious gift to give to someone. Listening encourages people to share their feelings and opinions. It demonstrates respect and caring. Listening can also help people to get to know one another as individuals, not as stereotypes. It can clear up misunderstandings. In this way, listening can resolve potential conflicts—before they lead to anger.

The following approaches will help you strengthen your listening skills.

Focus on the Speaker To most people in the United States, looking at the speaker is a sign of interest. (Lesson 15 will discuss cultural differences relating to eye contact.) In addition, we can turn our body so that it faces the speaker. This shows that we want to hear more.

We should ignore the television or any other people in the room and resist the urge to straighten papers or leaf through a magazine. We should try to put aside other thoughts and concerns. Our job at that moment is to listen.

MAKING A CONNECTION
TO LANGUAGE ARTS

Being able to hear is an immense help in communicating. However, many people who cannot hear have found other ways to understand others and to share their own thoughts and feelings.

Choose someone from the list below or another person you know (or know of) who has a hearing loss. Write a brief report explaining how this person communicates (or communicated) with others.

- Ludwig von Beethoven, composer
- Linda Bove, actress
- Bernard Bragg, actor
- I. King Jordan, president, Gallaudet University
- Helen Keller, lecturer
- Marlee Matlin, actress
- Heather Whitestone, Miss America, 1995

Ask for More Information Without interrupting, we can encourage the speaker to tell us more. We can do this directly by asking questions such as these:

- "And then what happened?"
- "How did you feel about that?"
- "Didn't that hurt?"

We can also encourage the speaker indirectly by making comments such as:

- "That sounds frustrating!"
- "I bet that was fun!"
- "That makes sense to me."
- "I see what you mean."

Leaning forward and nodding also are good ways to show that we are listening.

Paraphrase What You Hear To *paraphrase* means to "restate something in other words." Paraphrasing is an essential step in communicating, a way to see if we really understand what the other person is saying. It gives the other person an opportunity to say, "Yes, that's what I mean." We might also hear, "No, that's not quite it ..."

When we paraphrase, we summarize what the other person has said in our own words. If it seems appropriate, we might mention how the other person seems to be feeling.

If we state a paraphrase as a question, we are encouraging the other person to agree or disagree with it. Here are some examples:

- "You're worried about being cut from the team?"
- "You think your parents might be planning a divorce?"

To Do and Not To Do
• •

Of course, at the same time that we're using these good listening techniques, we need to avoid the kinds of responses that tend to block communication. You'll recall that these include interrupting, telling your own story, and giving unasked-for advice. You probably have a few other not-listening habits to add to this list.

Think about the people that you really enjoy being around. Chances are that most of them are good listeners. All of us appreciate good listeners, and all of us could become better listeners with a little effort.

Keeping a Journal

Choose someone in your life, at home or at school, and give him or her the priceless gift of good listening. Spend as long as it takes talking with this person about his or her day, any current problems, a coming event—anything that is important to that person.

Afterward, describe in your journal the person's reaction to your listening. Did he or she seem to talk longer than usual? Were you surprised at what he or she shared with you, once you took the time to listen? How can you apply this experience to your daily life?

TALK IT OVER

Work in groups of three to practice good listening. Decide who will be the first speaker, listener, and observer. The first speaker will choose a topic from the board. (The next speakers can choose a different topic or continue with the previous speaker's topic.) The listener will indicate physically and verbally that he or she is listening and wants to hear more. The observer will take notes on the listener's techniques.

After two or three minutes, the teacher will call time. Each observer will point out good techniques that the listener used. Then group members will switch roles so that everyone has an opportunity to practice listening.

THINK IT OVER

1. During the activity above, how did it feel to have someone really listen to what you had to say?

_____

_____

2. What did you do that was different from your usual habits when you had the role of listener?

_____

_____

3. What are some benefits for the speaker of good listening?

_____

_____

4. What are some benefits for the listener of good listening?

_____

_____

5. Look back at your answer to question 2 on page 51, on the qualities of being a good listener. Explain below how you might add to or revise your answer.

_____

_____

LESSON 14

Body Language

Bodies have a language all their own. You can tell at a glance who is listening and who is not. Your body talks to the people around you, even if you aren't saying a word.

You learned to understand body language at an early age, starting with Mom's frown when you pushed the jar of creamed peas off your high chair tray. After years of practice, you can tell when your parents or friends are having a bad day just by watching them walk toward you. Their facial expressions, posture, and gestures tell a lot about what's going on in their minds.

Nevertheless, as aware as they are of others' body language, most people often forget about their own. Your body language should help to communicate what you are saying. It should not turn others off or antagonize them. Your goal is to make others more aware of the whole message that you are communicating.

WHAT DO YOU THINK?

1. If one of the people in the left photo from the previous page said, "Tell me more," what would you think?

_____

_____

2. What messages are the people in the right photo from the previous page communicating through body language?

_____

_____

Interpreting Body Language

Do you think that teachers know which students are listening during class? Of course, they do. Even students who are giving oral reports know who is paying attention to them. They can tell from each person's eye contact, facial expression, and posture.

However, body language can be misleading, too. One behavior can indicate different emotions depending on the situation. Use what you already know about body language to fill in the blanks below. Write at least one word in each blank.

1. Posture

Slouching can mean that someone is bored. It can also

mean _____ .

Stiff shoulders can mean that someone is angry. It can

also indicate _____ .

2. Gestures

Drumming fingers on a table can mean that a person is

impatient. It can also mean _____ .

Arms crossed over the chest can mean that a person is

turned off. It can also mean _____ .

A tapping foot can mean that a person is angry. It can

also mean _____ .

Keeping a Journal

Take a "snapshot" of yourself at least three times during the next 24 hours. For example, you might be sitting in class, watching television, or talking with a friend or parent. Describe the situation, how you feel at that time, and what body language you are using.

Then review your notes. What do they tell you about your own body language? Do you use it often? effectively? Did it ever contradict what you were really feeling at the time?

3. Facial Expressions

A *smile* can mean agreement. It can also mean

_____ .

A *frown* can mean disagreement. It can also mean

_____ .

4. Eye Contact

Not making eye contact can mean that you are not listening. It can also mean _____ .

Staring at another person can mean that you are angry. It can also mean _____ .

5. Voice

A *high-pitched voice* can mean excitement. It can also mean _____

A *hoarse voice* can mean that someone is close to tears. It can also mean _____ .

Mixed Messages

• •

Stan is making himself a sandwich in the kitchen as his younger sister Melanie talks to him.

"Then I looked in my pocket, and my lunch money was gone!" Melanie says.

Stan stabs a table knife into the jar of peanut butter and pulls out a great brown glob.

"Stan! Did you hear what I said? I lost my lunch money!"

He looks over at her. "Huh? Oh, yeah. You lost your lunch money. Too bad."

"Then I had to ask the cook to give me lunch for free. She said she would, but I'd better ..." Melanie's voice trails off, but Stan doesn't seem to notice as he opens the refrigerator.

"You're not listening again, Stan. I can tell."

He begins to search for jelly. "Yes, I am, Melanie. I always listen to you. Go ahead."

What do you think that Melanie will believe: what Stan says or what his body language tells her? Sometimes your body can contradict the words that you actually say. The conflict between your words and your body language can lead to conflict in a relationship.

Making a Connection

to Drama

Work with two or three classmates to create a skit based on pantomime. Plan a way to use gestures, facial expressions, and other body language to act out a problem and resolve it.

After groups present their skits to the class, discuss the various types of body language that you used.

You probably have seen many examples of mixed messages. One is the person who smiles and says that she's sorry that she cannot do what you asked. Another is the classmate who agrees with your group's project plan but keeps his arms crossed over his chest.

Mixed messages can cause people to distrust one another. People do not believe words when bodies send a different message.

Does this mean that you should control your body language carefully when you say something that is not entirely true? Not at all. What it does mean is that people should express themselves honestly in the first place. In that way, your body language won't contradict you.

TALK IT OVER

1. With two or three classmates, compare how you answered the questions in the *Interpreting Body Language* activity on pages 57–58. Discuss the reasons for any differences in each of your interpretations of certain body language. Remember that people's cultural backgrounds influence how they interpret body language.

2. Discuss this question as a class: What are some things that you might do if a person's body language contradicts what he or she is saying?

THINK IT OVER

1. If you see a stranger use certain body language, can you be sure that you understand what it means? Why or why not?

_____

_____

2. What are some things that you could do if you notice yourself using contradictory body language?

_____

_____

3. Under what conditions might someone purposely use contradictory body language?

_____

_____

Communicating Across Cultures

Kent (thinking): *Joseph asked me if I liked the movie that I saw last night, so I thought he wanted to hear what it was about. Now he's acting as if he's bored. Why doesn't he look at me? Maybe I should go talk to someone who's more interested.*

Joseph (thinking): *I can tell that Kent is angry about something, but it can't be me. I've just been standing here, listening to him talk about the movie. Maybe I should say I have to go some place now. I could try to talk to him later, when he's not so mad.*

What's wrong with this picture? Kent expects Joseph to make eye contact to show that he is listening and interested. Joseph, however, is avoiding eye contact to show that he respects his friend.

Each teenager's culture has influenced how he communicates, but this misunderstanding is causing a conflict. If Kent and Joseph understood cultural differences that relate to communication, they might enjoy this conversation.

This lesson will help you become more aware of some cultural differences in communication styles. However, remember that the people within any culture are individuals. You cannot assume that all people from one culture will communicate in one particular way.

The traditions and attitudes of the cultures described in this lesson are meant to be points to consider. They are not specific descriptions of the unique people you will meet from these cultures.

WHAT DO YOU THINK?

1. Should Kent be angry with Joseph? Why or why not?

_____

_____

2. Will Kent be less angry if Joseph waits and talks with him another time? Why or why not?

_____

_____

Communication Customs

● ●

Our families teach us to talk, so the way that we communicate is strongly influenced by our families' cultural background. Although cultural differences tend to decrease as groups live in the same country for several generations, they can still cause misunderstandings. Below are areas in which our differences can lead to conflict—or make life more interesting.

Eye Contact A number of cultures consider the eyes to be the "windows of the soul." Yet this belief affects their customs about eye contact in different ways. European cultures, for example, tend to believe that they can understand others better if they look into their eyes. Thus, they consider eye contact a part of good listening.

On the other hand, Native American and Asian cultures teach that direct eye contact is disrespectful. This is especially true among people who do not know one another well. Looking into people's eyes to learn their emotions is like looking into their private lives. Besides respecting others' privacy, looking down or away is also a way to show respect for authority.

Keeping a Journal

The way that we greet people is strongly affected by culture. Write a brief description of how you greet your friends. What words do you usually use? What is your tone of voice? What kind of eye contact do you make? Do you touch your friends as you greet them? In what way? What have you seen others do as a greeting, but would feel uncomfortable doing yourself?

African Americans may use eye contact to indicate that they are ready to ask a question or make a comment. For some, looking away may be a sign of thinking, not disinterest. In Latino cultures, prolonged eye contact is used mostly with family members or close friends.

Personal Space During conversations, many people from European cultures tend to be comfortable with about 20 to 30 inches between themselves and others. This space keeps everyone at "arm's length" and shows respect. People from Native American and Asian cultures often stand farther apart, perhaps 24 to 36 inches. They may consider standing closer to be rude.

Latinos, on the other hand, may stand only 14 to 24 inches apart during conversations. While this may seem too close for other people, it is comfortable for many Latinos.

People from various cultures vary in the personal space that they need. Sometimes it depends on the emotional level of the conversation.

Touch Latinos are generally more comfortable than other cultural groups with hugging, patting, or kissing each other in public. People from northern European cultures are not likely to touch one another during a conversation, other than to shake hands. However, people from Mediterranean cultures may feel more comfortable about touching.

Among Native Americans, public touching tends to be rare. Their handshakes are often gentle and brief. Many Asians prefer bowing slightly to each other rather than shaking hands.

Gestures and Facial Expressions The use of gestures and facial expressions to communicate tends to follow the same cultural patterns as touching. Latinos often use gestures to express themselves. This is especially true when they are speaking in their native languages. Many people from European and African American cultures also speak with their hands. The more gestures they use, the more emotional is the conversation.

Gestures are not often seen in Native American and Asian cultures. The expression of feelings through gestures or facial expressions tends to be discouraged out of respect for others. Native Americans are also less likely to smile in greeting than are people from European and African American cultures. Yet a Native American who does not smile in greeting is not being unfriendly.

Keeping a Journal

List three or four "rules" that people from your culture generally follow when they communicate with others. These rules might relate to using eye contact and gestures, establishing personal space, and so on. Then list at least two things that you should consider when you talk with people from other cultures.

Among Asians, a smile can be used to mask other emotions. Thus, a smile can have many meanings, from happiness to disagreement.

Directness People from European cultures are probably the most direct of the cultural groups. They tend to speak their minds and feel comfortable bringing up a wide range of topics. Nevertheless, many still prefer to approach difficult topics indirectly.

African Americans and Native Americans might use stories and examples to bring up an emotional issue. Latinos, who tend to be very supportive of each other, often are uncomfortable offering bad news. Many people from Asian cultures feel that it is polite to put themselves down as they compliment others.

A Word of Caution

• •

Remember that the sections that you have just read do not accurately describe *all* of the people in the cultures named. They are generalities that become less true, as we all adjust to living with other cultures.

You may know shy people from European cultures and excitable people from Native American cultures. Each of us is unique. Yet it's still valuable to consider differences that do generally exist among people from various cultures. Becoming more aware of factors that can affect communication will help you identify possible misunderstandings. In that way, you can resolve them before they lead to conflict.

TALK IT OVER

With a group of classmates, discuss ways that people in your own culture tend to communicate. Explore which descriptions in this lesson you think are accurate and which are not. Choose one or two conclusions, and offer them to the class.

THINK IT OVER

Why should we consider individuals first and cultures second?

_____

_____

LESSON 16

Communicating Without Confusion

If that's the one you want to see, Ashley, it's okay with me."

Paul (thinking): *I wish that Ashley would pick some movies that have a little more action. I can stand to sit through another boring movie if that's what it takes to keep her happy. Maybe next week we could do something a little more interesting.*

Ashley (thinking): *I picked the movie last week, too, but Paul must have yawned twenty times while we were watching it. Maybe he'll be bored with this one, too. I wish he'd tell me what he really wants to see. I'm getting tired of trying to read his mind.*

Are Paul and Ashley headed for conflict? At this rate, their relationship probably won't last long enough for them to have a real argument. Paul is so eager to please Ashley that he agrees to anything that she wants. Yet, instead of making her happy, he is driving her away.

Few people, including Ashley, like to guess what another person really wants or needs.

Communication between Paul and Ashley is confused because of his unwillingness to say what he really wants. This lesson will help you sort out more of the verbal and nonverbal things that confuse communication—and often lead to conflict.

WHAT DO YOU THINK?

1. What could Ashley do to improve their communication in this situation?

_____

_____

2. Is Paul being respectful toward Ashley? Toward himself? Why do you think so?

_____

_____

Ways of Relating
• •

When you want something, do you always ask for it in the same way? Let's say that you need to borrow a dollar. How would you ask a parent for a dollar? How would you ask a brother or sister? Would you ask a younger brother differently from an older brother?

Few of us relate to everyone in the same way. In some situations, we are more confident. In other situations, we are less confident. Occasionally, we might become a little too confident and not treat others respectfully. However, we each have a general way of relating to other people. Such a style might be *passive, assertive*, or *aggressive*. The sections below describe these behaviors and show how some of them can lead to conflict.

1. ***Passive Behavior*** "Let me see your geography homework, Paul," Andy says, as he holds out his hand.

"Ah, well, I don't think…" Paul stares at his feet. He knows how convincing Andy can be. Then he remembers that Andy is friendly with Ashley. Maybe he should let Andy see his homework, just this once. Then maybe Andy will do him a favor and convince Ashley to go out with him again.

PUTTING WORDS TO WORK

- **Passive:** not taking an active role; putting others' needs before yours; allowing others to make decisions for you

- **Assertive:** expressing your needs and opinions with confidence but without attacking others; standing up for your own rights

- **Aggressive:** putting your needs before the needs of others; attacking those who do not agree with you

"Uh, Andy, you know Ashley, right?"

"Sure. Hey, is that your geography notebook?"

"Yeah. Uh, I wonder if Ashley's, uh, dating anyone?"

"I don't have a clue, Paul. C'mon, I just need the answer to the last problem."

Paul sighs. Why can't Andy understand what he wants? "Well, if all you need is one problem…"

Poor Paul. He's always so calm, and he never seems to get angry. He also never gets what he wants because he always assumes that other people's needs are more important than his. He assumes that other people can figure out what his needs are, if they want to.

Paul experiences "quiet conflicts" all day long. Often, other people don't even realize that he is having a conflict. That's because Paul can't bring himself to say what he really means—or wants.

2. Aggressive Behavior "Hey, Paul, this is just what I need! Thanks!" Andy grabs all of Paul's geography homework and stuffs it into his own notebook.

"But… but what am *I* going to turn in?" Paul protests. "It's due today! That… that's my only copy!"

"Paul, you're such a nerd! Just tell the teacher you lost your homework. She'll believe you 'cause you always do everything right. But she's going to be amazed at how hard *I* worked today!" Andy grins, turns, and pushes his way down the crowded hallway.

Andy has never considered anyone's needs but his own. Still, he can't understand why other people are so unhappy with him all the time. Teachers, friends, his family, even people he doesn't know—they're always complaining about some little thing that he did.

So he borrowed Paul's homework. Considering Andy's geography grades, he needed that homework more than Paul did. So what's the big deal? Why is everyone always on his case?

Andy's life is one unending conflict. The "little things" that he does have offended others, lost him many friends, gained him some detention, and even earned him a black eye or two. Yet he fails to recognize his own major contributions to these conflicts.

3. Assertive Behavior After geography class, Andy is sauntering toward language arts when he suddenly remembers that book reports are due that day. Luckily, he spots Ashley.

"Hey, Ashley!" He grabs her arm.

Keeping a Journal

Write about a situation in which you have communicated passively, not stating your own needs. Next, describe a situation in which you were assertive. Finally, describe a time when you might have been aggressive.

Now think about your usual style of communicating. Are you mostly passive, assertive, or aggressive? What, if any, problems has this caused for you? What could you do about these problems?

Ashley turns and eyes him suspiciously. "What's up?"

"Well, I was just thinking, Ashley, sweetie. You're the best writer in language arts, so Mrs. Hart loves you. I bet she won't even care if you don't turn in your book report today." He glances down at the report that she is carrying and grins.

Ashley looks him in the eye. "No way, Andy. I worked hard on this report, and I'm not giving it to you."

Ashley could have given in, like Paul did. Or she could have laughed in Andy's face when she realized what he wanted. Instead, she simply explained what she was not going to do.

Ashley's confident response stopped Andy in his tracks. He could tell that there was no point in insisting. Yet he didn't get angry because she didn't attack him. Ashley respects herself, and she also treated Andy with respect.

Communication and Conflict

Conflict often occurs when people have needs that are not being met. People who communicate passively, like Paul, often don't tell others what their needs are. Then they become angry when their needs aren't met. At the same time, their friends become annoyed at having to guess what the passive person really wants or needs. Instead of being resolved, the conflict has increased.

When people clearly but respectfully tell others their needs and limits, like Ashley did, they are communicating honestly. Any conflict between their needs is out in the open and can be discussed.

When Andy demands that his needs be met, no matter what, he invites others to become angry with him. He encourages conflict that can build to the point of a physical attack.

By communicating her needs and limits clearly, Ashley has avoided becoming part of a conflict. By not stating his needs or his limits, Paul has been drawn into several conflicts. (What is he going to tell the geography teacher about his homework? How is he going to feel every time he thinks about Andy grabbing his homework?) By insisting that others meet his needs, Andy moves from one conflict to the next.

Certain situations might call for passive, assertive, or even aggressive behavior. However, we need to consider whether our choice of behavior is helping us meet our needs—and how it is affecting others.

TALK IT OVER

Your teacher will divide the class into three groups. Each group should read the situation below. One group will describe how Chris might passively respond to Terry. One group will describe how Chris might respond aggressively. The last group will describe how Chris could respond assertively. Each group will describe both verbal and nonverbal behaviors.

The Situation: "Chris," Terry says, "I'm going to be in big trouble unless you help me. You've got to tell my parents that I was at your house last night!" Terry was not at Chris's house the night before.

A reporter from the "passive group" will read the group's responses to the class. Continue in the same way with the "assertive" and "aggressive" groups' responses.

Your teacher will collect the responses and distribute each to a group other than the one that produced it. Each group will write how Terry might react to the response that the group received. Groups will then share with the class how they imagine that Terry might react. Explore whether each response avoids or leads to conflict.

Sometimes it helps us be less passive, less aggressive, and/or more assertive if we think about our rights as

A Closer Look

These guidelines will help you avoid conflict by being assertive:

- Respect yourself. Remember that you have rights as a human being. Have confidence in yourself and in your own decisions.

- Respect others, including their cultures and values.

- Explain your needs without insulting or attacking others.

- Recognize when you are angry, and calm down before you try to deal with a problem.

- Hold your head high, and use comfortable eye contact when you talk with people.

human beings. Work with your group to list four or five rights that each person has. For example, one right might be the right to be respected. Then share your list of rights with the class. Create a master list, and post it. This can help everyone remember not only his or her own rights, but those of others.

THINK IT OVER

1. What kinds of body language show that a person is passive? aggressive? assertive?

   Passive: _____

   _____

   Aggressive: _____

   _____

   Assertive: _____

   _____

2. How might a passive person become more assertive?

   _____

   _____

   _____

3. How might an aggressive person become more assertive?

   _____

   _____

   _____

4. What are some advantages of being assertive?

   _____

   _____

   _____

Summing Up

- Interrupting, telling your own story, and giving advice are behaviors that discourage people from talking to others. These and other poor listening habits can lead to conflict.

- Good listening means focusing on the speaker, asking questions, and paraphrasing what you think the speaker said. These skills can improve communication and avoid conflict.

- Body language can speak as loudly as words. Be aware of the messages in your body language.

- Learning about the communication styles of other cultures can help avoid misunderstandings.

- Assertive communication avoids conflict, while passive and aggressive communication encourages it.

Applying Ideas

State whether the situation below is an example of communicating in order to avoid conflict. If it isn't, describe the problem and a solution.

Situation:

"I just found out that my family is moving at the end of the school year," J.D. told Danielle.

"Hey, we moved last year," Danielle said. "We used to live in Cincinnati, you know."

"I'm really going to miss everyone at this school."

"Nah! You'll make new friends right away. I did!"

Is this good communication? _____

Why or why not? _____

_____

How could it be improved? _____

_____

_____

_____

Exploring the Basics of Conflict Resolution

"I know your article's not in there, Hank. We just didn't have room for it this week," said Karen carelessly. "Maybe next time."

"You had room for everything that you and your friends wrote!" screamed Hank. "Maybe if I wore the 'right' clothes or hung out with the 'right' kids, my article would be in here!"

These two people are definitely having a conflict. Hank worked hard on his article, but Karen doesn't seem to care. At the same time, Hank's attack on Karen is greatly increasing the level of tension between them. Hank and Karen could have avoided this angry exchange. All that they needed were the listening and other communication skills that you will learn in this unit.

LESSON 17

Walking in Others' Shoes

Think about what might be happening in this picture. Write several sentences about what might be happening.

_____

_____

_____

Share your ideas with two or three other students. Even though you all looked at the same picture, did you all reach the same conclusions? Probably not, unless your backgrounds and experiences are very similar.

Maybe the students in your group are all the same gender, come from the same culture, have the same religion, and have always lived in the same neighborhood. In that case, your descriptions of the picture might be similar.

Even then, each of you is unique. You each still might have described the picture differently because each of you looked at it from your own perspective. You applied your past experiences and assumptions to this situation. Then you guessed.

This lesson will help you understand how our different perspectives can make life interesting, but can also lead to conflict.

WHAT DO YOU THINK?

Do you think that your group's descriptions of the photograph would have been more similar if you could have seen the whole picture? Why or why not?

_____

_____

_____

Points on Perspectives

• •

Let's say that five people are standing at five different windows at your school. Each is going to explain what he or she sees outside. Each is standing in a different position, so each description will be different. One might describe the parking lot; another might describe the sidewalk leading to the front doors; another might describe the building next door. These people each have a different physical point of view. Their points of view affect what they see.

Each of us also has a different mental point of view. It affects how we view things. Your mental point of view—or perspective—is based on everything that you've ever seen, experienced, been told, or imagined. Your point of view on a topic is a summary of everything you know—or think that you know.

Sometimes we are so sure that our point of view is "right" that we do not consider other possibilities. Suppose that one of the people looking out the window shuts her eyes. She says that she doesn't need to look out the window because she already knows what's out there. What's more, she can describe every pothole in that parking lot.

Suppose that she had come into the building by a different door than usual. She hadn't noticed that the gymnastics team was using the parking lot to practice for the state finals. In this case, she is missing a new experience. Likewise, if we're sure that we know what's happening in the picture on page 72, we may close our minds to other possibilities. We might also draw some incorrect conclusions.

Before we act in any situation, especially a conflict, we should make sure that we have all of the information that we need. That means keeping our eyes—and our minds—open.

PUTTING WORDS TO WORK

- **Assumption:** a guess, opinion, judgment, or conclusion
- **Perspective:** a point of view or a position from which you consider or evaluate something
- **Misconception:** an incorrect belief or conclusion or a wrong impression
- **Stereotype:** an assumption about a group of people or a belief that everyone in a group is identical

Stereotypes

Science class has just started. Groups are getting ready to present their projects to the class.

"I'm ready to read my report," Angel tells Kamal and Kathleen. "But where's Gordon? You know, I bet he never made those diagrams!"

"Huh! I bet he got lost on the way to school," Kamal says. "Now how are we going to present our project?"

Kamal knows that Gordon receives special help with reading. Based on this information, Kamal has stereotyped Gordon as a slow-learner who shouldn't be in his class. In fact, Gordon will be there soon. He is waiting for the school's media specialist to make his diagrams into overhead transparencies.

When Gordon finally rushes into class, he is surprised to see his group members frowning at him. Just as Kamal opens his mouth to say something, the teacher, Mr. Fermi, asks the group to make its presentation. Later, Mr. Fermi tells the group that he raised its grade for the project by half a letter because of Gordon's excellent diagrams.

Stereotypes and Blindfolds

Many times each day, similar conflicts take place at school, at home, and at work. In fact, they occur everywhere that a person's actions are shaped by stereotypes. Stereotypes are like blindfolds that shut people's eyes to the uniqueness of everyone around them. They allow people to jump to conclusions based on mistaken ideas. People who stereotype think that they know what a certain person is thinking, or what someone will do or will not do. These assumptions keep people from resolving conflicts.

To resolve a conflict, you need to keep an open mind and consider all the possibilities. For example, take Gordon's lateness. Kamal assumed that Gordon had not completed the diagrams. He almost blamed Gordon for ruining the group's project.

Kamal's assumption was based on his belief that people with mental abilities that are different from his are not capable. He assumed that Gordon would not be able to do his part for the project. Fortunately, Kamal discovered his mistake before he could act on it.

When you find yourself in a conflict, you need to make a real effort to find out, *not assume*, what the other

MAKING A CONNECTION

TO ART

Draw or paint the same object from two different perspectives. For example, you might draw it from one side and from the top—or from close up and from a distance.

Then describe the object from both of these perspectives. How does it seem to differ, depending on your perspective? What does this tell you about conflict?

person wants or needs. You must put aside stereotypes and keep an open mind. You actually need to take a few steps in the other person's shoes. Sometimes that's not easy, but the next lesson offers some ways to do this.

TALK IT OVER

Attach two pairs of paper footprints to the floor, facing each other. Two students will choose one of the statements below, and one will stand in each pair of footprints. One will have two minutes to speak in favor of the statement. The other will speak for two minutes against it.

After both have spoken, the students will trade places and stand in each other's footprints. Then, they will explain each other's viewpoint. Continue with other students and other issues. Afterward, discuss what this activity shows about walking in others' shoes.

- The minimum age for a driver's license should be 18.
- The wolf in the story of "The Three Little Pigs" (or "Little Red Riding Hood") was just misunderstood.
- Boys and girls should attend separate schools.

THINK IT OVER

1. Why is it sometimes difficult for us to "walk in another person's shoes"?

_____

_____

2. Why is it important to remember that other people may have different experiences, values, and needs than we do?

_____

_____

_____

3. How can believing a stereotype keep someone from understanding another person's viewpoint?

_____

_____

Listening With Empathy

"And then everything slid right off my tray onto the cafeteria floor!" Sheila felt her face get hot again as she thought about it.

"You know, Sheila, that happened to me once," Lee told her, "only the cafeteria was really crowded, and we had soup that day. You should have seen how far that went! But I just got another tray and pretended nothing happened. That's what you should have done."

"That must have been pretty embarrassing," Martin said. "Did anyone help you clean up the mess?"

Cassie snickered. "Maybe you need ballet lessons or something to improve your coordination, Sheila."

Good listening is a gift that many people do not know how to give. Sheila is upset and hoping for some support from her friends. However, not all of them are ready—or able—to give her what she needs. The embarrassment that she feels may soon turn to frustration or even anger.

Lee and Cassie need to work on improving their communication skills. Anything that improves communication also reduces conflict. You learned the basics of good listening in Lesson 13, but listening in a sensitive situation requires more than basic skills. It requires the ability to identify the feelings behind someone's words and understand his or her point of view. Sometimes empathy is all it takes to avoid or resolve a conflict. This lesson will help you learn how to listen with empathy.

WHAT DO YOU THINK?

1. Which teenager's response would encourage you to share your feelings? Why?

_____

_____

_____

2. What would annoy you about the other two responses?

_____

_____

_____

Finding Feelings

· ·

Lesson 17 stressed the need to understand the other person's point of view during a conflict. But how can you do that? First, consider what you already know about this person. Think about his or her background, goals, and concerns. You can find out more about other people by watching, listening, and asking questions.

In a sensitive situation, you must be particularly careful to avoid roadblocks to communication. These include: interrupting, telling your own story, giving unasked-for advice, and saying one thing but sending a different message through body language. Instead, you need to show with your body language that you are interested and listening.

Your questions and comments can encourage the other person to talk about his or her feelings. For example, you might say:

- "What bothered you most about his comment?"
- "That must have been frustrating."
- "You sound kind of discouraged."

PUTTING WORDS TO WORK

- **Empathy:** understanding someone else's feelings or point of view but not necessarily sharing or agreeing with those feelings or that point of view
- **Sympathy:** understanding and sharing someone else's feelings

Paraphrasing can be very helpful in empathic listening. It allows you to determine whether you understand what the other person has said. For example:

- "So you think that...?"
- "What I hear you saying is..."
- "Do you mean that...?"

While you're asking questions, however, you must choose carefully. Avoid questions that are too personal or off the subject. For example, suppose that Martin had asked Sheila, "Did you cry? Remember that time you almost cried in math class?" These kinds of questions would probably discourage Sheila from talking any more about this embarrassing situation.

Probing for the Problem

You can often uncover a conflict by asking the right questions. For example, suppose a group of four students is planning a class trip. Shaun suddenly says: "Go where you want. I'm not going to offer any more suggestions."

B.J. might respond, "Okay, let's go to St. Louis." If B.J. were really listening, he would have heard the anger behind Shaun's words. At this point, Shaun might leave the room and not come back.

Karen might say, "Relax, Shaun. We can't do everything your way." Again, Shaun might leave the room, angrier than ever.

But what if Robin asked: "Do you think we're too critical of your suggestions, Shaun?" Robin would have stated what she guessed that Shaun was thinking. Now he has the opportunity to confirm her guess or explain what he really is thinking. Either way, she has opened a door that may keep this conflict from going any further.

TALK IT OVER

1. With your group, study the situations below. For each one, think of a response that would encourage communication and one that would discourage communication. Then choose one situation, and share both of your responses with the class.

   Situation A: Karl says, "I didn't know you changed the meeting time from 4:30 to 5:00. I had to beg my brother for a ride to get here by 4:30."

Keeping a Journal

Think about a recent situation in which you really would have appreciated an empathic listener. Describe the situation and the actual responses (or lack of response) you received from others.

Then write the dialogue you would have liked to happen. Afterward, write another sentence or two explaining any insight that you gained from this journal entry.

Situation B: Beneka says, "I've never tried that before. You'd better ask someone else to help you."

Situation C: Antonio says, "I want to write letters to the people at the nursing home, not go there and visit them."

Situation D: Mia says, "I just read our group report, and a section that I wrote was missing."

2. Working with a partner, choose a situation below. Then write a dialogue in which one person uses empathic listening to better understand the other person's situation and feelings. Make up details if you wish. Several pairs will act out their dialogue in front of the class.

Situation A: One partner has not been invited to a party being given by his or her former best friend.

Situation B: One partner just missed being chosen for a sports team.

Situation C: One partner has found out that a parent is moving out of the family's home (or has a serious illness).

Situation D: One partner has discovered that his or her girlfriend/boyfriend went out with someone else.

THINK IT OVER

1. Why should listeners not be too quick to give advice?

_____

_____

2. How can stereotypes interfere with empathic listening?

_____

_____

3. How can you have empathy with someone even if you don't agree with him or her?

_____

_____

4. What are some situations in which you could use empathic listening?

_____

_____

_____

Explaining Yourself

"Lisa, you tore my favorite sweater. It's ruined! You never take care of my stuff. I'll never lend you anything again!" cried Monica.

We don't need to use empathic listening to identify the problem here. The cause of this conflict is clear, and Monica has a right to be upset. Yet, does a torn sweater have to end their friendship?

Monica is expressing her anger in a way that will severely strain their relationship. She is blaming and attacking Lisa. Lisa will need a great deal of patience and self-control to stop herself from attacking Monica back.

Yet, it is possible for Monica to express her feelings assertively and honestly without attacking Lisa. If she does, their friendship may survive this unpleasant incident.

This lesson describes a way that we can tell others that we are angry or annoyed—and resolve problems instead of making them worse.

WHAT DO YOU THINK?

1. What is a positive way that Monica could express her anger?

_____

_____

2. Does Monica's way of communicating seem passive, assertive, or aggressive? Why?

_____

_____

Communication Starts with "I"

· ·

Bottling up angry feelings is always a temporary way to deal with them. They don't just go away. Sooner or later, the angry feelings will boil over—or even explode.

However, just blurting out what you're thinking is rarely the best approach. Instead, try to express your feelings and thoughts in a way that does not attack or blame the other person.

"I messages" provide a framework for doing this. For example, "I feel...(name how you feel, such as frustrated, disappointed, worried) when you...(explain exactly what is bothering you) because...(tell why this action bothers you)."

(Some "I messages" also explain what you would like the other person to do. However, if you want to explore possible solutions with this person, you might skip that part of your "I message.")

For example, instead of attacking Lisa, Monica could have said, "I feel angry that you returned my sweater with a tear in it—it's my favorite sweater."

Now Lisa has a chance to apologize and to offer to repair the tear or replace the sweater. The girls can remain friends. Even if Monica attacks Lisa, Lisa can still use an "I message" to express her own feelings. For example, Lisa might say: "It hurts when you put me down like that because I didn't even realize that your sweater was torn. I wish you would give me a chance to explain my side of the story."

"I messages" help us organize our responses, but no one has to use this framework exactly. Notice that Lisa said "it hurts" instead of "I feel hurt." She also might have said: "I don't like being yelled at. I didn't even

Keeping a Journal

Try out an "I message" in the next day or two. Instead of swallowing your feelings or blasting someone with them, express them with an "I message."

Then describe the situation in your journal. Explain what you would usually say or do in that situation, and what you said or did instead.

Describe how the other person reacted. Did the problem get better or worse? What might have happened if you had responded as you usually do?

realize your sweater was torn." No matter what words you use, try to focus on the other person's specific actions and how they affect you.

People can become angry when they are attacked or blamed for something. However, they are much less likely to become upset if they know how their actions affect others.

More Than "I"

Some people assume that any sentence that begins with "I" or "I feel" is an "I message." Here are some that are not "I messages":

- "I want you to stop being so obnoxious."
- "I think that you are lazy and inconsiderate."
- "I feel that you are wrong."
- "I feel certain that you did this on purpose."

Each of these statements still manages to blame the listener. A true "I message" does not blast someone else.

Passive and Aggressive Messages

Lesson 16 explained passive, assertive, and aggressive responses. "I messages" are assertive responses. They show that you respect yourself and others. In addition, no one has to guess how you feel about a problem.

A passive message might be silence—no message at all. Of course, keeping a lid on your anger doesn't get rid of it. This anger may burst out at the worst possible time. On the other hand, some people think that they should say nothing if they can't say something positive. Still, forcing others to guess your feelings does not lead to strong friendships.

A good assertive "I message" can still be wasted if the speaker uses passive body language. Passive Paul might stare at the floor and mumble, "I feel frustrated that you didn't tell me that the meeting time was changed. I missed my ride home, and there isn't even a meeting today." Paul's body language, however, says: "Keep ignoring me. I'm not important, and I know it."

An aggressive response might be called a "you message." Here are some examples:

- "You ruined my sweater!"
- "You embarrassed me!"
- "You never do anything right!"

A Closer Look

"I messages" work well between people who are about the same age or between teenagers and younger family members. However, it may not be appropriate for a teenager to use an "I message" with an adult family member, a teacher, a coach, or others. In many cultures, this direct expression of feelings might be considered disrespectful.

"I messages" may also be inappropriate when someone is threatening you. (Lesson 21 discusses bullying.)

Aggressive responses often lead to more aggressive responses, and then to major battles.

Of course, using an "I message" doesn't guarantee that the other person will stop annoying you. However, most people will try to change a behavior or a situation that bothers others.

TALK IT OVER

Work with a group to list as many words as you can that describe feelings. Here are some examples to get you started: *resentful, disgusted, homesick.* Combine the groups' lists into a class list. Then each group will choose two feeling words from the list, make up conflict situations to go with them, and write an "I message" using each word. Share your messages with the class.

THINK IT OVER

1. Tyrone borrowed Jonathan's math book but forgot to bring it to school the next day. Jonathan said to Tyrone: "Where is your brain, Tyrone? Can't you remember anything? How am I going to take my math test today, huh?"

   Evaluate Jonathan's response. If you can improve it, write what he should have said.

   _____

   _____

   _____

2. Juanita was not invited to Carl's party. Now she has learned that Carl didn't invite her because Stephanie had said that Juanita would be out of town over the weekend. Juanita says to Stephanie: "I feel furious that you are butting into my life. Mind your own business from now on!"

   Evaluate Juanita's response. If you can improve it, write what she should have said.

   _____

   _____

   _____

LESSON 20

Encouraging Calmness

"Are you trying to kill me, Pete? That ball came within an inch of my head! My little sister can throw better than you can!" Kenneth yelled.

This conflict has quickly slipped past the stage at which these two teammates could have calmly talked about that wild pitch. Kenneth's anger rose so fast that there was no time for empathic listening or for expressing feelings with "I messages."

The excitement of the game and the pressure to win had already pumped extra adrenaline into Kenneth's bloodstream. Now, a close call with a hard ball has sent his emotions into overdrive. He is using some of his extra energy to attack Pete—verbally at this moment, but perhaps physically in a minute.

The level of tension in this conflict is rising rapidly. Anger is hard to control when a situation reaches this stage. This amount of anger is also likely to lead to violence.

Lesson 10 suggested a number of ways such as taking a deep breath and counting to ten, that Pete could get his own anger under control. Believe it or not, Pete could

also help Kenneth calm down before this situation goes out of control. This lesson includes techniques that you can use to help others calm down when they reach this stage. When everyone is calm again, conflict resolution can take place.

WHAT DO YOU THINK?

1. During a conflict, what actions or attitudes can cause other people to get angrier?

_____

_____

_____

2. What are some signs that a person is getting angrier?

_____

_____

_____

When Others Are Hot...

• •

Some conflicts can be resolved by making an effort to understand the other person's perspective. Yet, at times, the other person's perspective is clear, but the conflict remains. Sometimes you can quickly settle a conflict by assertively telling another person what is bothering you. But sometimes you won't get this opportunity because the other person is already too angry to listen.

In these tense situations, it's always helpful to remain calm yourself. However, you also need to have special "tools" available—techniques to help other people cool down so that no one gets hurt, emotionally or physically. As you read over the list below, think of times when these "tools" might be useful for you.

Ask for More Time Time apart can give everyone an opportunity to cool off and think about the situation. You might say, for example: "Let's talk about this later, okay? I need some time to think (or calm down)." Then you can bring up the subject later. Otherwise, it can seem as if you're avoiding the issue, not asking for more time.

You should also be careful about how you suggest a delay. For instance, suppose you say, "Let's talk about this later—when you aren't acting so crazy." This kind of comment insults the other person and adds fuel to the fire.

A Closer Look

The word RELATE can help you remember the skills from these units and deal with conflicts.

Recognize the signs that you're becoming angry.

Examine what you're telling yourself about the situation.

Listen to the other person.

Ask questions in order to understand his or her point of view better.

Try to stay calm.

Express your feelings without attacking the other person.

Agree with the Other Person Instead of arguing with the other person, find something to agree on. Agreeing with even one small thing that the other person says will relieve some of the tension in the situation. For example, you might say:

- "You're right. I was late."
- "I shouldn't have done that."
- "I should have called when I said I would."
- "That's true. I do need to work harder on that."
- "It probably does seem that way to you."

Make a Joke Sometimes a joke can lighten up the situation. Remember when Kenneth suggested that his little sister could pitch better than Pete could? Pete might have responded, "That's good news! Can she pitch in tomorrow's game?" This unexpected response could give Kenneth a chance to think about what he's saying and calm down a little.

A joke can show that the situation isn't worth getting so angry about. At the same time, making fun of the other person's feelings or needs will greatly increase the tension.

Apologize It's possible to apologize without accepting the blame for a situation. You can apologize for a situation that has resulted in the other person becoming angry, hurt, or disappointed. When people realize that others care about their feelings, they often feel less angry. For example, you might say:

- "I'm sorry that what I did made you so angry. Are we still friends?"
- "I didn't think this would happen. I'm sorry."

Use Calm Body Language If you're in a conflict, be sure to speak slowly and calmly, and stand a comfortable distance from the other person. Relax your muscles, and try not to wave your arms around. The calmer you seem, the calmer the other person is likely to become—as long as you don't seem to be unconcerned about his or her feelings.

Suggest a High-Energy Activity When your emotions are rising, so is the adrenaline in your bloodstream. You have to get rid of that excess energy. You might suggest playing a fast game of basketball, running, doing some aerobics—anything to use up energy. The other person doesn't even have to know why you're suggesting it. Even if you exercise by yourself, at least one person will feel calmer.

Leave the Situation Suppose none of these techniques seems to help, and the other person is still very angry. Then the best thing to do is to leave the situation if possible. All this anger may lead to violence if you stay. If necessary, ask an adult for help with the situation.

Being Prepared

• •

Often, you can predict that others will have angry reactions to your words or actions, such as when you are disrespectful. Thus, you can avoid certain words and actions that are sure to lead to conflict. Being respectful saves wear-and-tear on everyone.

Yet, sometimes people unexpectedly become angry. The cause can be a difference in perspectives, past experiences, or cultural backgrounds. The cause can also be a simple misunderstanding, such as confusion about the time of a meeting. You can't always predict the causes. Still, when they occur, you need to be prepared to help everyone involved, including yourself, to cool down. Then you can sort out the conflict calmly.

TALK IT OVER

With your group, brainstorm a list of common conflicts that young people face. Then match each conflict with a technique from this lesson that might help the people involved to cool off. Share your conflicts and cooling-off techniques with the class. Afterward, discuss which suggestions from this lesson seem most helpful.

THINK IT OVER

1. Select a technique explained in this lesson, and identify a time when it might not be the best approach to use.

_____

_____

2. Under what conditions is anger likely to lead to violence?

_____

_____

Coping With Bullies

Molly announced, "If any of you goes and sits with Shelly, you'll be the next one sitting by yourself all the time!"

Who says only boys can be bullies? Bullies can be boys or girls or men or women of any cultural group or nationality. In this case, Molly is using words to dominate the girls sitting with her. However, some bullies use physical violence—or the threat of violence—to control others. Bullying is a form of aggressive behavior carried to the extreme.

Bullies cause conflict wherever they go. Yet, they tend to be immune to the approaches that the previous lessons suggest for avoiding and/or resolving conflicts. Bullies' interactions with others are attempts at control, not communication. Thus, good listening is not likely to uncover a need that can be easily met. Bullies themselves are not good listeners and tend to lack empathy. They cannot imagine—or do not care—how the other person feels.

Responses to bullying have to be chosen carefully because many bullies are looking for an excuse to be

violent. Nevertheless, there are some recommended approaches that can help you deal with bullies while staying safe. The suggestions described in this lesson will also help protect a common victim of bullying: your self-confidence.

WHAT DO YOU THINK?

1. How do you think the girls sitting with Shelly feel?

_____

_____

2. What are some physical or nonverbal behaviors that you consider to be bullying?

_____

_____

3. What are some verbal behaviors that you consider to be bullying?

_____

_____

Recognizing Bullies
● ●

There are several types of bullies. Even in elementary school, some bullies are so aggressive that both adults and classmates avoid and dislike them. These bullies encourage other people to reject them. Then they use this rejection as proof that others are against them.

Since bullies are certain that others are out to get them, they make a point of attacking first. This may be the type of bully who ends up convicted of crimes when he or she is older.

Another type of bully is admired by his or her classmates—in a nervous sort of way. Molly is this type of bully. She presents herself as a leader, an important person to know and to please. However, she controls others by threatening them with isolation—with not being part of the "in-group." This is a serious threat to young people who are eager to fit in and to belong to a group.

Molly will keep her power as long as her victims are too frightened to stand up to her. Thus, Shelly isn't Molly's only victim. The other girls sitting with Molly are also her victims.

A Closer Look

- Nearly 90 percent of elementary and middle school students and 80 percent of high school students report being bullied at school.

- Most bullies can be identified on their first day at school.

- Bullies who are allowed to continue intimidating others are five times more likely than their classmates to be convicted of crimes.

Targets and Bystanders

Bullies usually select their targets carefully. At school, they may single out classmates who are different in some way, perhaps physically or culturally. They look for people who are not likely to stand up to them or who become very upset when they are teased. Bullies might choose someone who's new at school or someone who prefers solitary activities. These kinds of targets usually do not have a large circle of friends to support them.

Bullies may torment people just for entertainment. Or they might do it to show their followers what will happen to anyone who gets out of line.

Bullying tends to make even bystanders nervous. They know that they might be the next victim. Bystanders may laugh or smile to please the bully. However, by not objecting, they make the bully's behavior seem acceptable or even entertaining.

Dealing with Bullying

Each situation is unique, so the guidelines below offer various ways to respond to bullying. Not all of them will work in every situation. Consider, in particular, your physical safety. If the situation involves weapons, a gang, or out-of-control anger, for example, the best approach is to leave if at all possible.

If you are the target of a bully:

- Ignore the teasing, and walk away. Stay in control. Bullies hope that you will become upset. If you stay calm, they may lose interest.

- Laugh along with the teasing. When you're laughing instead of blushing, you don't make much of a victim.

- Explain your feelings about the situation. Calmly use an "I message". This approach may not work with some bullies. However, some people have just never considered others' feelings. They may be surprised to learn how their behavior is affecting you and may decide to stop the teasing.

- State your limits. Use assertive behavior to describe what you will and will not accept. For example: "I'm not letting you see my homework today." You may have to repeat this several times until the bully gets the message.

Keeping a Journal

Think of times when you have seen people being bullied at school. In your journal, describe one situation that especially bothered you.

List three things that you could have done then or later to help the target or to get the bully to stop. Remember, your goal is to keep yourself and the target safe.

- Do not allow a bully to control you or make your decisions. If any of the girls on page 88 had gone to sit with Shelly, Molly's power over all of them would have been broken.
- Ask friends for their support, such as walking with you to school. However, do not let this become one gang against another. If the situation continues, ask an adult for help.

If you are a bystander:
- Assertively express your feelings about the situation. For example: "When you tease May Lee about her accent, I feel bad because I know how hard she is working on her English. I would like you to stop teasing her."
- If you know someone is being bullied, offer your support. If a situation is getting out of control, ask an adult to help.

TALK IT OVER

Work with your group to identify a common bullying situation at your school. (Do not name specific people.) Then think of at least two ways that the target person could handle it and one way that someone who is not directly involved might help. Share the situation and your ideas with the class. Then discuss whether your school has a significant problem with bullying and intimidation.

THINK IT OVER

1. How do you think bullying affects the target?

_____

_____

2. Imagine that someone is trying to bully you into doing or not doing something. What are at least two positive messages that you could give yourself in this situation?

_____

_____

_____

_____

Summing Up

- Being aware of various perspectives can help you avoid or resolve conflicts. Remember that everyone's life experiences are different.

- Empathic listening can help you learn how others feel. It can enable you to understand other perspectives better.

- Express your feelings and opinions honestly, without attacking or blaming the listener.

- You can often help others calm down during a conflict.

- Dealing with bullying requires special approaches.

Applying Ideas

Read each situation below, and apply what you've learned in this unit. (Read over the RELATE suggestions on page 85 before you begin.)

Situation A: You and C.T., your best friend, planned to go to the mall this afternoon. You just found out that C.T. has invited someone else to come with you. Lately, C.T. and this other person have been together a lot—without you. You consider staying home—or accusing C.T. of having a new best friend. What are some positive things that you could do about this situation?

_____

_____

_____

Situation B: One of your teammates grabs your arm in the hallway between classes and shouts, "I know you told the coach what happened last week! Now he's going to kick me off the team!" You did talk to the coach today, but not about this person. How could you best handle this situation?

_____

_____

_____

Putting the Basics Together

"You need another half hour? I have language arts in half an hour! Can't you let me use the computer, just for a few minutes? Please?"

Conflicts such as this one occur often. Heather is panicked because she needs to finish her language arts report before class starts.

Eric is trying to finish his own language arts report, but he can't concentrate with all the noise that Heather is making. *If she would just leave me alone,* Eric thought, *I could write my summary and be out of there.*

These two people need to resolve this conflict before one of them says or does something that he or she might regret. They need to understand each other's needs, to think of possible solutions to meet those needs, and to choose a solution that both can accept.

If Heather and Eric knew about the problem-solving approach to conflict resolution, they could find a way to settle this conflict. This unit will show you a step-by-step way to resolve conflicts.

Negotiating Solutions to Conflicts

"Jake," Reuben said, "come and get in line. Phil and I really want to see this movie."

Jake has already seen that movie, and it wasn't very good. Still, he wants to spend some time with his friends. So Jake is faced with a conflict. As in most conflicts, he has three choices: ignore the conflict, confront it, or problem-solve.

These three approaches are similar to the three types of communicating that you read about in Lesson 16. If Jake is passive in his relationships, he will probably avoid this conflict and just get in line with his friends. That's easier than arguing, he might tell himself. The movie wasn't *that* bad.

If Jake is an aggressive type, he might try to get his own way by putting down the movie and/or his friends. For example, he might say: "Only geeks want to go to this movie, Reuben. C'mon, you two geeks. I'm going to save you from yourselves. I've got a really cool movie picked out."

Fortunately, Jake is usually assertive. This means he will try to resolve this conflict in a way that everyone involved can accept. How will he do it? It's not that difficult. This lesson will show how you can resolve conflicts and still keep your self-respect—and your friends.

WHAT DO YOU THINK?

1. Why are conflicts like the one that Jake faces so common?

_____

_____

_____

2. What's the problem for Jake if he goes with his friends to the movie that they picked out?

_____

_____

_____

3. How might Jake's friends respond if he takes an aggressive approach?

_____

_____

_____

Kinds of Conflict
• •

Conflict is normal and happens every day. It can happen any time that two or more people of any age live or work or do anything together. Yet, not all conflict is negative. In fact, conflict can be valuable. Facing conflict can force us to consider what is really important in our lives. Resolving conflict can result in positive, needed changes. Conflict can even strengthen our relationships—if those involved resolve it in an acceptable way.

Most conflicts can be placed into one of these three categories:

- A conflict over *things*: two or more people want the same thing, but there isn't enough for everyone.
- A conflict over *needs*: two or more people have needs that conflict. Perhaps one person needs to feel powerful, while the other needs to feel respected.
- A conflict over *opinions or values*: two or more people disagree about what is right or best. This can range from a conflict in religious beliefs to a conflict in movie preferences.

MAKING A CONNECTION
TO SOCIAL STUDIES

Just as nonverbal language varies from one culture to another, different cultures also tend to resolve conflicts in different ways. In some cultural groups, for example, a conflict between two people must be resolved by their families.

Work with a small group to find out how conflicts are resolved in a certain culture. (You might talk with older relatives in your own culture.) Then, write a report or show the class how a typical conflict would be settled. Do remember to show respect for other people's traditions and customs.

How Not to Handle Conflict

No matter what kind of conflict we face, certain approaches work better than others. Just as each person develops a way of communicating, each person also develops a way of handling conflict. Our way of communicating greatly influences how we handle conflict.

During a conflict, Passive Paul keeps his eyes on the floor. He doesn't try to explain his point of view or his feelings. Instead, he may apologize for whatever happened, even if he did nothing wrong. He is so uncomfortable that he doesn't use his listening skills to try to find out how the other person feels. He just stands there with his head down, ready to escape as soon as he can.

Aggressive Andy doesn't listen either. He doesn't care what anyone else thinks. Andy matches his loud demands with angry gestures. His gestures are designed to discourage others from voicing their opinions. Andy interrupts others whenever he feels like it.

Positive Problem-Solving

KC has lost Ashley's sunglasses and can't afford to replace them. Assertive Ashley uses the skills that you have read about in this book to resolve this conflict and save her friendship with KC. Here are the steps that she takes:

1. *Get Ready*

First, Ashley does her best to forget any past disagreements with KC and to focus on today's problem. She takes a few deep breaths to clear away any angry feelings. Then she asks herself if she is ready to handle this. If she were still too angry, she would tell KC that she wants to talk about the sunglasses later, when she is calmer.

2. *Listen*

Ashley listens carefully to KC's side of the conflict and asks questions. She repeats what she thinks KC said in order to see if she really understands KC's point of view.

3. *Explain*

Then Ashley uses an "I message" to explain her needs: "I feel angry that you lost my sunglasses because I need them for the baseball game tomorrow." As she speaks, Ashley stands tall and confident, looking KC in the eye. She doesn't blame KC for being careless, and she doesn't act disgusted.

Think about the problem-solving approach outlined in this lesson. Describe in your journal how it is different from the way you usually resolve a conflict. For example, do you skip the calming-down step? the brainstorming-together step?

Now think about a conflict that you often face. Describe how the problem-solving approach might help you resolve this conflict.

4. *Brainstorm*

Now that Ashley and KC understand each other's point of view, they think of possible solutions to the problem. The solutions might include: KC buys Ashley new sunglasses, or Ashley borrows her sister's sunglasses for the game, or Ashley buys herself new sunglasses.

5. *Discuss*

Ashley and KC discuss the possible solutions that they've listed. Then they reject any that one of them does not like or cannot accept. For example, KC doesn't have any money right now, so she rejects buying new sunglasses for Ashley. Ashley rejects borrowing her sister's sunglasses.

6. *Choose*

Ashley and KC choose the solution that will probably work best for them: Ashley will buy her own sunglasses, and KC will pay her back each week from her allowance.

Most conflicts can be resolved quickly. This is possible if both people listen carefully and explain their needs without attacking each other. However, when good communication doesn't settle the conflict by itself, the problem-solving steps listed above can help. It doesn't take long to follow these steps. Five minutes may be enough time to identify a solution that everyone can accept. In the next lesson, you'll have an opportunity to try out these steps.

TALK IT OVER

With your group, list three guidelines or attitudes that will help people resolve their conflicts. One might be: "Forget stereotypes." Create a class list, and post it.

THINK IT OVER

1. Which of the six steps for problem-solving given above do you think many people skip?

_____

_____

2. Why is it important to think of many possible solutions?

_____

_____

Practicing Conflict Resolution Skills

"Sequoia, you said that you'd help me with my math tonight!"

"Well, I was going to, Anthony, but I have a report that's due...."

"You said you would!" He held up his math book. "I don't know how to do this stuff!"

"Anthony, you're in fifth grade. I'm in high school. My school work is a lot more important...."

"Not to my teacher! You always treat me like a baby! You don't think that anything I do is important!" Then he turned and yelled, "Mom! Make Sequoia help me!"

Do conflicts seem to follow you around some days? Do they find you at school, at home, maybe even in your own kitchen? Knowing how to resolve these everyday conflicts can take the rough spots out of your day. However, you have to be ready to use the skills that you've learned in these units. This lesson will give you some practice in using the problem-solving approach to conflict resolution.

WHAT DO YOU THINK?

1. What did Sequoia do to raise the level of tension in this conflict? What did Anthony do?

_____

_____

_____

2. Write an "I message" that Anthony could have given to Sequoia after she first told him she was too busy to help him.

_____

_____

3. Now write an "I message" that Anthony could have given to Sequoia after she pointed out that she is older than he is.

_____

_____

Picking Our Fights

• •

Besides knowing the steps in problem-solving, we need to know when to use them. Some conflicts are too trivial or unimportant to bother with. For example, let's say a good friend of yours is excited about something. He has interrupted you several times during a conversation. You might feel annoyed, but you probably would ignore this conflict.

However, suppose someone has accused you of playing poorly during a team sport. Instead of ignoring this comment, you might ask questions and listen carefully to find out what is actually bothering the other person. Or you might express your feelings about the comment with a clear, honest "I message."

In a third kind of conflict, suppose that you are part of a large crowd leaving a city-wide basketball game. Your team won a very close game, partly because of a referee's call. The other team's fans are angry. Suddenly, someone shouts an insult about your team. A few others in the crowd cheer. This situation could be dangerous. This is definitely not the time for careful listening or for an "I message." Instead, you need to leave as soon as possible.

Keeping a Journal

Think about the conflicts in your life. In your journal, describe:
- a trivial conflict that you should ignore (whether or not you usually do ignore it).
- a troublesome conflict that is interfering with your relationships and that you should try to resolve peacefully.
- a dangerous conflict that you should avoid.

Putting Skills to Work

• •

Now it's time for you to practice applying the problem-solving approach. Read the conflict situation below, and write what you would do for each step. You can work with a partner if you wish. (If you need help, reread the steps that Ashley followed in Lesson 22.)

Situation: Your brother (or sister), who is about your size, constantly borrows your clothes without asking. This morning you were planning to wear your last clean shirt to school, but your brother/sister beat you to it. He/she was on the way out the door before you were awake enough to recognize your shirt. You had to wear the same shirt to school that you wore yesterday. You borrow your brother/sister's clothes sometimes, but this has got to end!

1. *Get Ready*

_____

_____

2. *Listen*

_____

_____

3. *Explain*

_____

_____

4. *Brainstorm*

_____

_____

_____

5. *Discuss*

_____

_____

6. *Choose*

_____

_____

Keeping a Journal

Review the skills and ideas that you have gained from these units. Write at least three things you want to remember to do the next time you are in a conflict.

Then list at least three things you want to remember not to do during your next conflict.

Coping with Conflict

• •

Being able to resolve conflicts peacefully is an important skill in today's world. If anyone needs proof, the daily newspaper and evening news are full of examples of how *not* to resolve conflicts. Since each conflict is unique, we need to be familiar with several ways to resolve conflicts. This will help us choose the best approach for each conflict.

After a little practice with the skills in these units, you will be able to handle most conflicts on your own. However, the next lesson describes ways that young people can help each other resolve conflicts.

TALK IT OVER

Work with a group to apply the problem-solving steps to one of the conflicts below. Then share your process with the class.

Conflict A: Three weeks ago, Carol broke up with Ken. Ken has started dating other girls but wants to get back together with Carol. After thinking it over, Carol is willing to date Ken again, but she wants him to stop dating other girls.

Conflict B: Ron and Regina are assigned to do a science project that is due on Monday. Ron wants to work on it after school because he and his family will be out of town this weekend. Regina has cheerleading practice after school and wants to do the project over the weekend.

THINK IT OVER

1. What are some benefits of conflict?

_____

_____

2. Why is it important to distinguish between trivial and important conflicts?

_____

_____

_____

Using Peer Mediation

"Rachel, what do you want Brooke to do or stop doing?" asks Chelsea.

"Well, every time I walk past her, she stares at me, real mean-like. Sometimes her friends do, too."

"So you want her to stop staring at you, right?"

Rachel nods, and Chelsea turns to Brooke. "Brooke, what do you want Rachel to do or stop doing?"

"She told everyone that I was trying to take her boyfriend away from her. I don't even like him! I want her to stop saying that!"

Is Chelsea, the girl in the middle, just being nosy? Not at all! She's a peer mediator for the school's Mediation Center. Rachel and Brooke have been sent to the center. A teacher found them arguing in the hallway. Other students come to the center on their own. All are frustrated by conflicts that they haven't been able to settle. They know that another student will calmly help them settle it fairly.

Peer mediation is called "conflict management" in some schools. During peer mediation, trained students help other young people deal with their anger and explain their points of view about their conflicts. Then the mediator encourages them to think of possible ways to solve their conflicts. As a last step, they agree on the best solution.

In most cases, mediators enter a conflict only if asked, either by the people involved or by school staff. Some schools, such as Chelsea's, have set up special mediation centers. Other schools assign mediators to hallways, cafeterias, playgrounds, or other areas where conflict is likely to occur.

In this lesson, you will learn more about peer mediation. Even if you do not use peer mediation or become a peer mediator, the tips in this lesson will help prepare you to resolve your own conflicts peacefully.

WHAT DO YOU THINK?

1. Is the conflict between Rachel and Brooke important? Why or why not?

_____

_____

2. What skills or attitudes do you think a peer mediator should have?

_____

_____

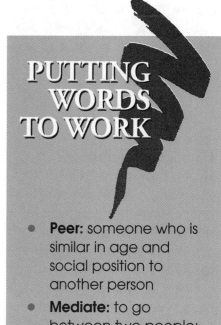

PUTTING WORDS TO WORK

- **Peer:** someone who is similar in age and social position to another person
- **Mediate:** to go between two people; to act as a referee or an umpire
- **Mediation:** the process of helping two people resolve their conflicts

Taking Steps

• •

The process may vary from school to school, but in general, peer mediators:

1. make sure that everyone involved wants to resolve the conflict.

2. invite each person to describe the conflict from his or her point of view.

3. restate what each person said, encouraging both people to add more information.

4. ask what each person wants the other person to do or stop doing.

5. ask if each person is willing to do or stop doing what the other person asked. Anyone who answers "no" must explain why not and must state what he or she is willing to do instead.

6. ask if each person if they can accept what the other agrees to do. If so, they shake hands and/or apologize.

7. ask the people involved whether they think that their conflict is resolved or whether an adult should be asked to mediate.

Mediation in Action

• •

Most peer mediators complete ten or more hours of training to prepare them to help others. Jeffrey is an experienced mediator, so let's see how he mediates a conflict between Manuel and Quincy. (The steps in the process are pointed out.)

Jeffrey: Why did you two come here? (Step 1)

Quincy: Manuel has no sense of humor. I thought you could help him lighten up.

Manuel: I have a sense of humor, all right, but I'm sick of yours, Quincy! (turning to Jeffrey) I'm hoping that you can persuade me not to smash his face in!

Jeffrey: I'll try, but what is the problem? Manuel, you seem to be the most upset. You go first. (Step 2)

Manuel: Quincy here, who has a pretty strange name himself, keeps calling me "Manny" when I told him a hundred times not to.

Jeffrey: You're angry because Quincy calls you "Manny"? (Step 3) (Manuel nods.) Quincy, what's your side of this?

Quincy: I can call him anything I like. Just because Manny—whoops! I mean Manuel—is a starter on the team doesn't make him a hero.

Jeffrey: You're angry because you think Manuel keeps the ball from you during games?

Quincy: I guess.

Jeffrey: Manuel, what do you want Quincy to do or not do? (Step 4)

Manuel: Call me by my right name!

Jeffrey: Quincy, what do you want Manuel to do?

Quincy: I'd like some respect during the games.

Jeffrey: Quincy, could you call Manuel by his right name? (Step 5)

Keeping a Journal

If your school does not have a peer mediation program, explain in your journal whether you think it needs one. What kinds of conflicts might this program resolve?

Then list two or three conflicts in your life that might benefit from peer mediation. If no mediation is available, what also could you do?

Quincy: I guess it wouldn't kill me, if it's that important.

Jeffrey: Manuel, could you show Quincy more respect at the games?

Manuel: I didn't know I was ignoring him during the game. (turning to Quincy) What do you want me to do?

Quincy: Just toss me the ball once in a while?

Manuel: (nodding) I could do that. No sweat.

Jeffrey: Are you each satisfied with what the other one is willing to do? (Step 6) (Both nod.) Do we need to get the coach or anyone else involved in this? (Step 7)

Quincy: Nah, we're okay now, right, *Manuel*?

Manuel: Let's go over to the court and see how good a player you really are!

The Causes of Conflict

• •

The conflict between Quincy and Manuel was really about respect, as many conflicts are. Quincy felt comfortable enough during peer mediation to explain what was really bothering him. Maybe Quincy hadn't even realized why he felt the need to harass Manuel.

Could Quincy and Manuel have resolved their conflict without a mediator? Probably, but sometimes it helps to have a "referee" keep everyone calm and talking. That's what most conflict resolution involves anyway—talking. Sometimes talking causes conflicts, but it almost always takes some careful talking and listening to resolve them.

TALK IT OVER

For this activity, your teacher will divide the class into groups of four. Each group of four will then break into two teams. One team in the group will pretend to have a conflict. The other team will work together as mediators to help resolve this conflict. Then, several groups will volunteer to explain one team's conflict to the class and to show how the other team helped resolve it.

THINK IT OVER

Why do you think that peer mediators need special training?

_____

_____

Summing Up

- A step-by-step approach can help people in conflict better understand each other's needs. It can also make it easier to meet those needs in a way that everyone can accept.
- Being able to resolve conflicts takes strong communication skills and lots of practice.
- Peer mediators can often help people calmly identify the cause of their conflicts and find positive ways to resolve them.

Applying Ideas

Apply the problem-solving steps to this conflict: Your older sister, Hollie, is supposed to take you to your team practice every Saturday morning at 8:30. On Friday night, you overhear Hollie tell your mom, "I have to be at work tomorrow at 8:00 A.M."

1. *Get Ready*

_____

2. *Listen*

_____

_____

3. *Explain*

_____

_____

4. *Brainstorm*

_____

_____

_____

5. *Discuss*

_____

_____

6. *Choose*

_____

Glossary/Index

Adrenal glands: two glands located near the kidneys that help the body respond to anger or stress; they also have other functions, 35

Adrenaline: a hormone released by the adrenal glands, 35

Aggressive: putting your needs before the needs of others; attacking those who do not agree with you, 65

Anger: a natural emotion that we may feel in response to events out of our control, others' attitudes or actions, our own attitudes or actions, our thoughts about any of these, 19

Assertive: expressing your needs and opinions with confidence but without attacking others; standing up for your own rights, 65

Assumption: a guess, opinion, judgment, or conclusion, 23

Bias: a preference for one thing over another, preventing fair judgment; prejudice, 7

Communicating: exchanging knowledge and information, 49

Conflict: natural disagreements that occur because we all have different values, needs, interests, and opinions. Conflict can occur with or without anger, 19

Discrimination: denying some people the rights or benefits that others have, 7

Empathy: understanding someone else's feelings or point of view but not necessarily sharing or agreeing with those feelings or that point of view, 77

Hearing: detecting sound waves, 49

Hormones: chemical messengers produced by glands and circulated in the bloodstream; hormones control many body functions, 35

Listening: using techniques that will help you understand what the other person is saying, 49

Mediate: to go between two people or to act as a referee or an umpire, 103

Mediation: the process of helping two people resolve their conflicts, 103

Misconception: an incorrect belief or conclusion; a wrong impression, 73

Nonverbal: without using words, 49

Passive: not taking an active role; putting others' needs before yours; allowing others to make decisions for you, 65

Peer: someone who is similar in age and social position to another person, 103

Perspective: a point of view or a position from which we consider or evaluate something, 73

Prejudice: liking or not liking someone or something without a good reason; prejudging people based on an assumption about the group to which they belong, 7

Racism: believing that people of a certain race are inferior, 7

Stereotype: a standard mental picture of a whole group of people; believing that everyone in a group is identical in certain ways, 7, 73

Sympathetic nervous system (SNS): the part of the nervous system that controls smooth muscles, such as those in the digestive system, and blood vessels, 35

Sympathy: understanding and sharing someone else's feelings, 77

Talking: saying words, 49

Verbal: using words, 49